TRUCK STOP
POLITICS

UNDERSTANDING
THE EMERGING FORCE OF
WORKING CLASS AMERICA

TOM MULLIKIN

Vox Populi Publishers, LLC
100 North Tryon Street, Suite 4700
Charlotte, NC 28202-4003

10 9 8 7 6 5 4 3 2 1

ISBN 978-0-9790178-3-4
        978-0-9790178-4-1

Printed in the United States of America.

CONTENTS

iv

DEDICATION

I would like to thank my family for all their support and love over the many years of being in the field; to thank my wife Virginia Ann and my children Mary Elizabeth, Alex, Thomas Jr., and Charlie for your strength and encouragement; and to thank my parents for instilling a strong work ethic, a sense of patriotic duty and love for our great Nation.

I would also like to thank my many political mentors who have helped me through the years. Starting with the former Speaker of the House in South Carolina, Bob Sheheen, who taught me to speak directly and listen to the concerns of the working man and woman. To former United States Senator Fritz Hollings, from whom I learned the need to master the substance of an issue before engaging. Senator Hollings' political instincts are unparalleled and helped me hone my own skills. Thanks to my first boss after college, Congressman John Spratt, from whom I learned a work ethic and the necessity of spending long hours mastering the difficult issues. To former Vice President Al Gore, whose analytical skills pushed me harder to understand the broader policy issues. And to my good friend John McCain, whose character is a constant reminder to speak honestly, directly and in the best interests of the United States of America. Senator McCain may be the greatest American of our generation and I am proud to list him as a friend. And finally to Juanita Tate, former head of the Concerned Citizens of South Central Los Angeles, who taught me to be bold enough to reach out to all working Americans and courageous enough to love with your whole heart. Ms. Juanita was an inspiration, and her lessons are ones which I can only hope and aspire to meet. To these and many more friends under whom I have had the amazing good fortune to study and learn, I deeply appreciate their support.

For my understanding of domestic industrial concerns, I want to thank my close friend and mentor Bob Johns. Bob's tutelage over the years has allowed me to raise my awareness of the important industry implications of political actions. I want to give special thanks to Dan DiMicco, whose courage and leadership of domestic manufacturing has given real meaning to my love for our government and the opportunities afforded to the working class in our great country. For a cripple boy born to a working class family in eastern North Carolina, were it not for the abundance of opportunities afforded to our working families, my life would have been vastly different.

To these and all of the many local and state "field" leaders with whom I have worked, I thank you for your support and for keeping the American dream alive. With your leadership our families can meet and overcome even the greatest challenges associated with the new globalization.

Lastly my warmest thanks to my team for helping prepare this manuscript, including my partners Nancy Smith and John Saydlowski, and my close associates Todd Muldrew and Peter "Rock" Allen. Taking an ol' redneck boy from the eastern Carolinas and trying to translate his thoughts into substantive (and readable) prose has been a job.

God Bless the United States of America!

FOREWARD

As a political scientist student in college, I had a teacher's assistant once tell me that if you couldn't sell your message in two minutes at a truck stop it was either wrong or wouldn't work. That T.A., Lee Atwater, went on to manage the successful presidential campaign of President Ronald Reagan, and to become the head of the Republican National Committee, where he helped craft policy that made sense for both the working man and woman of America and the corporate executive.

During the last dozen years, we have witnessed the enormous failure of our representatives in the District of Columbia to embrace the challenges of a globalized economy. These are challenges that American workers across our nation are able and willing to meet and overcome, if our leaders in D.C. allow us the opportunity.

Since my college days over twenty-five years ago, I have preferred working in "the field." My focus groups are the truck stops, barbershops, and small businesses of down-towns; from Kern County, California, to the Iron Range of Minnesota; from the Finger Lakes of Western New York, to the bayous of Louisiana. These are where Americans work and live. Unsuspecting politicians are about to learn that this vast constituency – working America – is rapidly coming to grips with the realities of globalization. Just a word of caution for those D.C. sycophants who prefer the illegal trade tactics of some foreign countries and multinationals – the sleeping American giant is waking, and it will realign American politics to meet this new challenge.

This book is written about the industrious American worker; a worker that neither prefers a Red state nor a Blue state, but a Red, White, and Blue state, where he or she can earn a living and leave for their children the same great legacy that was handed down to them.

TRUCK STOP
POLITICS

UNDERSTANDING
THE EMERGING FORCE OF
WORKING CLASS AMERICA

TOM MULLIKIN

PART 1

DEGREES OF SEPARATION

"Through our scientific and technological genius, we have made of this world a neighborhood . . . . We are tied together in the single garment of destiny, caught in an inescapable network of mutuality. And whatever affects one directly affects all indirectly."

— Dr. Martin Luther King, Jr., "Remaining Awake Through A Great Revoltion," March 31, 1968.

According to the hypothesis framed by the term "Six Degrees of Separation," any person in the world can be connected to any other person through a chain of no more than five people.

But in fact, there is only one degree of separation between any citizen and every elected leader of our nation: the vote. Each vote directly connects us with each person elected to represent us in our government.

But there is another kind of interconnectedness between individuals: the convergence of the interests and concerns of people who may only have a few things in common, and yet these common interests are fundamental to how they live their lives.

In the pages that follow, I focus on the common goals of Americans who make up the broader working class, including the blue collar workers who constitute a pivotal and highly influential part of the working class. Politically, we often focus on the one degree of separation (one vote) between each member of the working class and our elected leaders. The greater challenge comes with how we face the social and political connectedness between and among the diverse members of the working class voters.

Hardly surprising, given that the members of the working class number in the tens and tens of millions.

But the fact that they have not in the recent past coalesced as a voting bloc around a core of issues has perhaps aggravated the fractured and divided aspects of our political landscape. Different candidates, parties and interest groups angle for working class votes from every conceivable direction. Their success in carving away slices of this electorate may be found in issues that are based on social issues, foreign policy, religion, race, and others.

All of that has changed. Beneath the surface of American politics, pressure is building on working class Americans: job security, earning power, vanishing pensions, and widespread "social insecurity" about medical insurance and the afford-ability of basic health care. The effects of these changes travel outward from the individual workers, to their families, and through their communities. As more and more communities struggle to cope with the economic and social stresses of changing economic reality, the tension mounts throughout American society. The experts of "wedge politics" were wrong in 2006, and they will continue to be wrong until the broader concerns of working class Americans are addressed.

Right now people are still arguing over the health of the economy and the meaning of spiraling trade deficits, shuttered factories and an unprecedented global auction of jobs to the lowest bidders. But if the recent midterm elections were any indicator, American politicians are facing a day of reckoning, as millions of working Americans find that their common concerns have brought them much closer together and sharply reduced their degrees of separation.

As inaction by elected officials continues to jeopardize the future prospects of working Americans, the voting power of America's working class will continue to unify behind issues that will remake the American political landscape.

If our elected officials recognize the gathering storm, and seek change in measured steps and incremental progress, we might see relatively orderly realignments in our political parties and systems. But if current trends continue and are not effectively addressed, then the pressure could build – like the pressures that build deep below the surface of the earth until such time as the ground snaps and we are left to confront an earthquake – and one that leaves the old landscape as we knew it unrecognizable. If Washington responds to the needs of the working class, history may record the 2006 midterms as the shift that awoke our federal officials to the issues that working Americans have in common. If they fail to do so, history may regard these elections as the first pre-quake tremor.

PART 2
THE AMERICAN WORKER – THE PERSONAL LANDSCAPE

"The Declaration of Independence derived its peculiar importance, not on account of what America was, but because of what she was to become; she shared with other nations the present, and she yielded to them the past, but it was felt in return that to her, and to her especially, belonged the future. . . . So it is peculiarly incumbent on us here today so to act throughout our lives as to leave our children a heritage, for which we will receive their blessing and not their curse."

— Theodore Roosevelt, July 4, 1886, Dickinson, Dakota Territory

The personal landscape of the American Worker has never ceased to change. In contrast to more conservative cultures, Americans have reinvented their work and their workplace at such a pace that grandparents may be hard pressed to step into jobs performed by their grandchildren. We are dynamic people with a dynamic culture, and we are master navigators of the ever-changing workplace.

American workers do not fear change. They create change. But at various times in our history American workers have recognized the need to grapple with change and to make sure that change serves their interests and keeps this nation on a course of progress. With Americans, the velocity of change is not always as important as the direction of change.

Having said that, the opening decade of the new century finds American workers confronting changes that they openly and rightly question. Do these changes serve workers' interests? Do they keep the United States on a course of progress? Answer "yes," and the American worker responds with hard work, ingenuity and common purpose. Answer "no," and expect the American worker to question, to resist, and ultimately to steer things in a new direction.

Just a few generations ago the American worker looked like a farm hand. With the industrial revolution the American worker started to look more like "Joe Lunch Pail," with a job in a factory or a foundry, and a steam whistle that told him when to come to work, when to eat lunch and when to head home. Today he may be a she, and she may be a blue collar worker in a high-tech environment – making obsolete a lot of the old job descriptions and categories that applied to our national work force in general and the blue collar or working class work force in particular.

But for all the change and upheaval, some things are more constant. Working class Americans expect a fair day's pay for a fair day's work. They expect their hard work to earn a certain measure of financial security and family health. To the extent that "the system" falls short, we can expect them to work hard to change the system. If the American worker does not like the way things are headed then the leaders of the political and business establishment should expect action and reaction. They should expect social and political movements to call for a change of leadership and a change in direction.

Today, when the American worker surveys the landscape, how does it look? How broad is the horizon, how level the ground? A growing body of evidence suggests that all is not well with the American worker. Many see a red flag waving in front of the Blue Collar Bull.

The recession of 2001 got the 21st century economy off to a rocky start, and its lingering after-effects have combined with broader social and political trends to reshape fundamentally the landscape for working men and women.

For example, the recession and its effects are linked in the minds of many with the economic fallout from globalization, including offshoring, and the proverbial "race to the bottom" in terms of global wages, benefits and workplace protections. Never again will a U.S. recession be perceived as a local phenomenon, and the workers who are affected by these recessions are likewise expanding their world view and their political philosophies to account for this fundamental change in the landscape.

It is interesting to note that the U.S. Government is just now beginning to get its arms around the export of American jobs. As recently as 2004, in a report to the U.S.-China Economic and Security Review Commission, Dr. Kate Bonfenbrenner and Dr. Stephanie Luce reported "there is no government body that collects information detailing the incidence of production shifts out of the U.S. to China or to any other country."[1]

But of course, American factory workers do not require government statistics to show them the lay of the land. They have their pink slips, their interrupted earnings and the shuttered factory down the street to remind them of this economic dislocation.

And of course there are the daily encounters with manufactured goods formerly tagged, "Made in the USA" and now tagged "Made in Anywhere But."

How many workers have seen this same tag slapped on their jobs? How much are they feeling the effects in their jobs, their homes and their wallets?

With the wholesale offshore migration of jobs, the overall numbers often do not concern individual workers, but they should concern those who govern them. If current trends continue, then at some point the number of affected workers and their concerns grow large enough to become, in some way, a political or social movement.

Consider some of Dr. Bonfenbrenner's and Dr. Luce's findings. In one three-month period in 2001 they found 56 "shifts" of U.S. production from the U.S. to China, Mexico and India.[2] When they measured a similar three-month period in 2004 they tallied 255 production shifts to Mexico, China, India, Latin America, the Caribbean, Europe, Canada and several more Asian countries.[3]

It sounds somewhat clinical to discuss "production shifts." Here's how working men and women describe it: "The jobs are going away, and they aren't coming back." In this study, the jobs totaled 48,417 moved offshore, and it was estimated that the total for 2004 would approach 406,000 jobs, compared to 204,000 jobs in 2001.[4]

The researchers described the jobs as representing a "cross section of industrial sectors" and described the companies moving the jobs as "large, publicly held, highly profitable and well-established." Seventy-two percent of the facilities were owned by American multi-nationals.[5]

A 2005 study conducted by Sharon Brown and James Spletzer of the U.S. Bureau of Labor Statistics profiled that agency's first steps to measure the export of American jobs and reported that 90 percent of the establishments that had reported mass layoffs and moved work out of the country were in the manufacturing sector.[6]

The corporate and political leaders of this country would be well advised to see these jobs, these companies and the American economic system through the eyes of the American worker. Consider: as the pace of job exports accelerated following the end of the last recession, it contributed to the status of the recovery as a "jobless recovery." Each factory closing and layoff was duly reported in the local media, then combined in regional and national media in coverage of the broader trend.

This demonstrates how the economy is fundamentally different from, say, the war in Iraq in shaping workers' views of the landscape. If media coverage focuses on layoffs and the economy, Americans can examine the coverage in light of their own, local experience and judge if the media coverage is "getting it right." Not so with a war on the other side of the world, which is tangible only to those who are serving – or whose loved-ones are serving – in Afghanistan and Iraq. If local concerns about job loss are portrayed as part of a bigger problem, and enough people see this trend validated in their own back yard, then a consensus will begin to emerge that cannot be easily changed. The response of these workers at the ballot box is not a knee-jerk emotional reaction to a "wedge" issue. Job loss sparks a deep and visceral concern among these voters.

Bonfenbrenner and Luce reported that the greatest off-shore "shifts" in production came at the expense of workers in the Midwest and Southeast, with the two states of Illinois and Michigan suffering the most losses during the period covered by the study.[7] It is not difficult to perceive how the local landscape has been changed for the working people of those states. These states give us our first inklings of how political landscapes may change, as well.

The offshoring of jobs has proven to be a more ecumenical trend than experts initially predicted. At first, workers in some sectors of the economy were reassured that only the jobs of certain low-skill production workers were at risk from overseas low-wage competitors. But this proved to be false prophecy as the flood of jobs swept away not only manufacturing jobs, but information technology jobs, call center jobs and other occupations that were earlier regarded as relatively safe.

The myth commonly used to explain away these job losses is that what we are seeing is merely free market capitalism at work. Proponents argue that labor-intensive occupations are simply shifting to economies in the global marketplace that can provide the lowest cost labor. This analysis ignores the fact that foreign governments are playing a direct role in managing the market to create a multitude of incentives for business, often in violation of international trade laws. All American industries have been a victim of trading "partners" in Asia, Latin America and elsewhere that are employing a number of unfair and illegal tactics. Currency manipulation, prohibited by the World Trade Organization, is used by nations like China to fix exchange rates to keep their own exports cheap, and make American imports expensive. Intellectual piracy – and not just CDs and movies, but everything from electronics, to factory machinery, to prescription drugs – has been estimated by the U.S. Chamber of Commerce to cost American businesses over $250 billion a year, and a quarter of a million jobs to date.[8] State-owned banks in many developing nations provide billions of dollars in low-cost loans to facilitate the growth of national industry, and then forgive billions of dollars in bad debt, where U.S. lenders would take action to collect. These same governments will provide direct cash grants to their corporations, and intervene in negotiations between private parties to drive down the cost of raw materials. While American companies strive to provide some of the cleanest and most efficient production practices in the world, industries in developing nations thrive under non-existent or non-enforced environmental controls, and energy infrastructure that provides cheap but "dirty" electricity. Substandard workplace and labor standards allow local and multinational companies to exploit workers by paying below market wages and providing unacceptable working conditions.

Most of the almost 4 million American manufacturing workers who have lost their jobs know this. They have learned – at the cost of their jobs – how they have been deprived of their livelihoods in many cases by the illegal and unethical practices of overseas competitors. They also have

13

learned that their jobs have been replaced by offshore labor by companies that ostensibly share their American citizenship. Manufacturing workers have also become the standard-bearers for an American working class that is confronting diminished earning power for what may be the rest of their working lives.

August 2006 may fairly be described as "nondescript" in terms of employment data. The Federal Government's employment surveys of establishments showed that 128,000 jobs were created – not quite enough to absorb all of the job seekers coming into the market. On the other hand, hourly earnings rose just 0.1 percent, and for the 12 months previous had risen 3.9 percent, which was less than inflation. Also, hours worked and the length of the average workweek declined somewhat.

But a key factor in understanding the working class landscape is this: how are American workers doing at keeping up with inflation, nudging up their earnings, and working toward some degree of upward mobility or economic security? How well are they doing at providing for their families this year and for their old age security in years to come?

By now it is clearly established that simply counting the number of jobs in this country doesn't begin to tell the story. It is the *quality* and *kind* of job that matters to the American worker – whether you speak of the worker as an individual or as a class of people numbering in the tens of millions.

Consider these findings, reported by the Labor Research Association:

- By 2004, the ranks of the ten largest U.S. employers made the country look more like a nation of shoppers than a nation of producers, with five of the top ten employers being retail chains with relatively low wages. Wal-Mart had replaced General Motors as the largest U.S. employer, which does not bode well for worker pay when you consider that, at the time, a GM assembler earned on average about three times as much as a Wal-Mart employee.

- The shift of jobs from the manufacturing sector to the service sector has resulted in fewer opportunities for overtime pay, as more workers must take service sector jobs that employ a higher percentage of hourly and part-time workers. (The average hourly wage for a manufacturing job is $15.34, as opposed to $9.12 in a service sector job.) [9]

Another factor has been the relatively weak growth in jobs and demand for workers since the 2001 recession. The Economic Policy Institute (EPI) reported that employment grew by 1.5 percent in 2005 compared to an average of 3.1 percent employment growth during the same period in past recoveries.[10] Weak job growth, even after the decline of jobs finally ended in late 2003, has continued to depress wages. [11] The median wage increased 1.4 percent from 2000-2003 but declined 0.7 percent from 2003 – 2005.[12] Wages also declined for low-wage earners, with only high-wage earners seeing growth in wages during both periods.[13]

The National Association of Manufacturers in its 2006 Annual Labor Day Report pointed out that rising energy prices have significantly eroded Americans' ability to make ends meet.[14] The report said this:

"Rising energy prices are cutting into wages. While overall real compensation is rising, wages are not. The rising cost of benefits such as health care – which are continuing to consume a large portion of workers' pay checks – is partially responsible for the decline in real wage growth. However, the recent surge in energy prices is the main reason why workers' wages have not kept pace with inflation."[15]

The report went on to conclude, "This surge in energy prices has eaten into workers' paychecks and reduced their real wages. Since the end of the recession, real hourly wages have fallen 0.6 percent, while manufacturing real wages are down 1.7 percent."[16]

So this is the lay of the land: As workers have eked out incremental pay increases in the wake of the 2001 recession, they have seen much of this negated at the gas pump and when they pay their winter heating bill. A return to somewhat lower energy costs in 2006 has not fundamentally changed an energy market that is at such tight margins that any interruption or threat will send prices right back up. There is little optimism that the average worker can draw up a budget based on reasonable and predictable energy prices.

Another point of view says that the whittling away of the American paycheck is also due to such factors as increasing income inequality and a desire by some to channel more earnings into profits and less into workers' pay.

For example, the June 12, 2006 Economic Policy Institute Policy Memorandum cites the gap between wage increases and productivity growth. The EPI reported that productivity increased by 14.7 percent from the beginning of the post-recession recovery, but 46 percent of the income growth during that period was distributed as profits – compared to 20 percent in previous periods.[17]

Some might respond, "So what?" First, it is important to recognize that findings such as these are picked up by the mainstream press, find their way onto the internet and into newsletters by industrial, labor and other interest groups and eventually become part of the working class landscape. But to focus solely on the statistics is to overlook the fact that most workers have detected some evidence of this where they live and work. Both the statistics and the home-grown evidence are combined in the simple arithmetic that workers apply to corporate profits and their take-home pay: More for you is less for me.

"You" in this case may be perceived as any identifiable group that can be painted – fairly or not – as profiting at the expense of the American worker: multinational corporations, pharmaceutical companies, government "pork" projects, or any other convenient target. But if the average worker knows that she is having significant difficulties feeding her children, filling her gasoline tank and paying the rent, then it comes back to the perception that someone is gaining too much at her expense. This is the growing sensitivity of hundreds of thousands of working American families. This feeling is beginning to be understood by an Executive and Congress that has failed to give voice to the American worker (as opposed to the multinational campaign contributor).

If this perception hardens into an attitude and a deep-rooted point of view, then it is not unreasonable to expect political repercussions down the line.

In recent elections, politicians have decried "class warfare" strategies in local, state and federal races. The fundamental question for a political scientist is not whether "class warfare" is a legitimate tactic, but whether the political climate is such that this tactic can succeed.

In its 2006 edition of *The State of Working* America, the EPI reported that wealth inequality in America has grown significantly. In 1962 the richest 1 percent of "wealth holders" had 125 times the wealth held by a typical household.[18] By 2004 the ratio had grown to 190:1. [19] That is the difference between $82,000 and $14.8 million. The working class does not begrudge the wealth of the rich, so long as they are paid decent wages to provide for their families. This widening disparity is largely due to the failure of our nation's leaders to address the illegal actions of some foreign governments.

Irwin Stelzer, Senior Fellow and Director of Economic Policy Studies for the Hudson Institute, recently wrote this: "Something has been happening to the way the benefits of economic growth are being distributed in the United States. For reasons not fully understood, America's highest earners are garnering the largest share of the rise in the nation's income. At the same time, the relatively benign overall inflation figures mask the fact that the cost of living is rising more rapidly for the elderly (the price of drugs), than for the affluent young (think computers and flat-screen television sets). Result: a middle class that is beginning to question the American Dream that has done so much to ensure social stability, and that has typically rejected the appeals of leftish class warriors."[20]

Also during this time the American corporate CEO has become a standard bugaboo in discussions about paychecks. In 2005 a report titled "Executive Excess" was widely covered in the media when it reported that the ratio of CEO pay to average pay of production workers had grown to 431:1 in 2004 from 301:1 in 2003.[21] Although not a record, the report compared the ratio to the 1982 ratio of 42:1, which of course adds up to a more than ten-fold expansion of CEO pay relative to production workers. [22] This dynamic, alone, might well explain why many leaders of multinational corporations would prefer to forgo advocacy for enforcement of free trade agreements in favor or more malaise and refusal to seek free and fair trade. It is plainly a pattern of cheating to support blind individual greed.

But where such statistics really hit home is . . . home. Workers who struggle from paycheck to paycheck as single people feel a certain amount of pressure, to make ends meet or to try to scrape ahead just a little bit. But when you add in the family responsibilities of husband, wife, children, elderly parent, or other dependents, then the stakes are raised a hundred-fold – and so are the pressures, anxiety, frustration, resentment and all of the other emotions that are common to working people in these circumstances.

Let's look at the landscape from the perspective of working class families.

Real median household income in the U.S. rose by only 1.1 percent from 2004 to 2005, the first year since 1999 in which real median household income showed an annual increase – but still well below the rate of inflation.[23] Real median earnings of males 15 and older who worked full time, year round, declined 1.8 percent between 2004 and 2005, and women with similar work experience saw their earnings decline by 1.3 percent.[24]

Household incomes in various states ranged from a high of $61,672 in New Jersey to a low of $32,938 in Mississippi.[25] Twenty-eight states registered median incomes below the national median.[26] The average threshold of poverty in the U.S. for a family of four was placed at $19,971.[27] For comparison, note the earlier reference to the average annual pay of a Wal-Mart employee, at $18,000.[28]

From 2000-2004 real median family income fell by 3 percent, driven in large part by the jobless recovery following the 2001 recession, during which breadwinners experienced losses in jobs, hours and wages.[29]

Families faced the worst job recovery period following any modern recession during this time, when it took the economy 46 months to regain peak employment (compared to an average of 21 months for previous recessions).[30] Particularly hard hit were the high-wage jobs of the manufacturing sector, which suffered significantly from the ballooning U.S. trade imbalances and the export of jobs to Latin America and Asia.

According to the EPI's *State of Working America* report, when demographic changes in age and educational attainment are taken into account, the ability of the economy to generate good jobs has declined 25 percent to 30 percent over the past 25 years, with relatively strong growth limited to education, health services, financial services and construction.[31] Also, long-term unemployment as a share of total unemployment has grown substantially. In 1979, 8.6

percent of unemployed were long-term, but their share had more than doubled to 19.6 percent by 2005.[32]

What do all these statistics show? Regardless of how well the economy is doing overall, individual workers are working longer hours at more jobs for less money and fewer benefits. For a family to successfully confront both shrinking wages and diminished prospects of earning a paycheck, multiple wage-earners in the family must all contribute more. This creates stress in other aspects of personal finance and security.

Subtle pressures can be discerned by such findings as this: From 1979 to 2000, middle income wives in married couple families with children added more than 500 hours of work to total family work hours.[33] This may be seen as a glass half empty-glass half full statistic, depending on whether you are focusing on (potential) financial gain or the need to balance work and family. At this point it is not unreasonable to assume that it is both – that the family has received a certain financial dividend in order to keep up with the rising cost of living, but that stresses related to work and family balance have also emerged more urgently into the working class landscape.

Coverage by employer-provided health insurance declined from 69 percent of workers in 1979 to just over 55 percent by 2005, and workers are paying a larger share of insurance costs.[34] *The State of Working America* reports that of the total growth in premiums from 1992 to 2005, workers picked up half the tab.[35] And in a trend comparable to wages, the American economy enjoyed robust productivity growth from 1995 to 2005 (33.3 percent) but only a small portion of the health care tab has been picked up on behalf of workers (33 cents per hour for the period).[36]

The Labor Research Association reports that employers have been able to reduce the growth rate in health benefits costs from 10 – 12 percent per year in 2004 to 7 percent in 2006 through a combination of limiting coverage and a placing more of the cost burden on workers.[37]

Not surprisingly, the number of people (and costs) covered by taxpayer-funded health programs continues to climb.

The proportion of Americans who lack health insurance varies considerably from state to state. In Minnesota 8.7 percent of the population was uninsured on average from 2003 to 2005, in contrast with Texas where 24.6 percent of the population lacked health insurance during this time. Texas' high uninsured population may also reflect a higher immigrant population and the fact that 43.6 percent of non-citizens lacked health insurance in 2005.

Among developed countries, Americans pay more for health care than most, and 40 percent of adults reported in surveys that they chose to do without needed care because of high costs. Unlike other costs incurred by working Americans, the need to pay for health care brings serious financial stresses, profound emotional stress, and sometimes brings the imperative to choose between health and financial damage or ruin.

Meanwhile, from the textile factories to the gleaming skyscrapers of Enron in Houston, Texas, the American press has been afforded ample opportunity to shine the light on the relentless declines of The Great American Pension.

Working class families increasingly face the prospects of sharply reduced financial security after retirement, and indeed millions of people face the prospect of no retirement at all unless compelled by poor health and disability.

Along with health insurance, pensions are regarded as the employment benefit that has been subject to the greatest erosion or to outright elimination.

Today in the United States less than half of our workforce is covered by employer-provided pensions – about 45.4 percent. For men in the workplace the decline was from 56.9 percent in 1979 to 46.4 percent in 2004. Among lower-wage workers, only 14.3 percent were covered in 2004, and less than half of middle-wage workers were covered.

It is difficult to overstate the significance of this trend in the minds of working class Americans. Pensions – particularly among the traditional blue collar manufacturing and other good-wage sectors – became an important bond between employers and workers. They became perhaps the greatest tangible evidence of the social contract that once existed between American employers and workers: If you will commit your work, your career and your loyalty to us, we will compensate your years of service with pension income.

Today, when workers are forced to reassess their old assumptions about loyalty and economic security, there is no more powerful symbol of change than the abandoned American pension.

The pension was a cornerstone of the American dream that encouraged even working class people to aspire to the accumulation of wealth. This centered on buying a house and building wealth through real estate equity. It also included vested benefit pensions, savings accounts and other means.

But today in the paycheck-to-paycheck lifestyle, wealth is not accumulating. It is being siphoned away by debt, by insufficient wages, by layoffs and the interruption of careers, and all of the forces that continue to put upward pressure on the cost of living and downward pressure on the value of earnings.

In his Monetary Report to the Congress, Federal Reserve Chairman Ben Bernanke made headlines when he reported that the personal saving rate for Americans plummeted to a negative 0.5 percent for 2005. "All in all, personal outlays exceeded disposable income in 2005," he reported.[38] We now confront a significant "negative savings rate," which is FedSpeak meaning that Americans as a whole are not saving anything, we're just going deeper in the hole, continuing into 2006.

Bernanke also reported that household debt expanded at an annual rate of 10.5 percent during the first three quarters of 2005, or about the same "brisk pace" that was set in 2004.[39]

"Overall, the expansion in household debt outpaced the growth in disposable personal income," Bernanke reported.[40]

The U.S. Bureau of Economic Analysis (BEA) reported that U.S. personal saving for April 2006 had reached a "negative $146.8 billion" and compared it to the previous month's "negative savings" of $128.2 billion.[41] For the two months that meant that Americans were spending on average about 1.5 percent more each month than they earned.

The BEA dryly notes that, "Saving from current income may be near zero or negative when outlays are financed by borrowing (including borrowing financed through credit cards or home equity loans), by selling investments or other assets, or by using savings from previous periods."[42]

This seems to portray household budgets and a national economy living on borrowed money and borrowed time. Or as the old song goes, "another day older and deeper in debt."

The Labor Research Association reports that Americans are deeper in debt than ever before and that 14 percent of a family's *after tax* income is now required just to pay off debt.[43]

Americans' willingness (or necessity) to go deeper into debt has been either abetted or mitigated (depending on your point of view) by the rapid rise of real estate values and the equity that has accrued in people's residences.

The hot real estate market made headlines throughout 2005 and continued into 2006. In his report to Congress Bernanke indicated that sales of both new and existing residences set records in 2005, although new housing starts began to slow toward the end of the year as interest rates rose.[44]

Bernanke said that "uncertainty is centered on prospects for the housing sector. On the one hand some observers believe that home values have moved above levels that can be supported by fundamentals and that some realignment is warranted. Such a realignment – if abrupt – could materially sap household wealth and confidence and, in turn, depress consumer spending."[45]

For the upper middle class and wealthy this could amount to losses that are significant but that would still warrant nothing more drastic than mea culpas in cocktail party patter. But if a working class family has been compelled to borrow against the value of their house and the housing market tanks then the family could face the loss of the house and worse.

Can't happen?

Consider the case of Danville, Illinois, where real estate prices plunged 23 percent in the first six months of 2006. The reason? Major manufacturers continue to lay off thousands of workers across America, and Danville had the misfortune to be hit by multiple layoffs in a relatively short time.

While the overall perception across the country in 2006 continues to be upbeat for real estate and for the American home as a primary source of wealth, the National Association of Realtors Chief Economist Dr. David LeReah presented what he titled the "Real Estate Reality Check" at the organization's 2006 leadership summit.[46]

By the second quarter of 2006 the U.S. had become a "divided real estate nation," with contracting markets in 69 percent of the country and expanding markets in 31 percent.[47] LeReah reported that the "boom" ended in August 2005, and that rising mortgage rates and an erosion of affordability were transforming the markets.[48]

Speculators, resort buyers and "trade-up" buyers headed to the sidelines. And something characterized as a "high percentage of exotic loans" began to loom on the horizon. The report stated that 26 metropolitan statistical areas had price declines in the second quarter of 2006.[49] The rate of price growth for houses had plunged to about 1 percent from more than 15 percent in mid-2005, and during that same time condominiums went from 15 percent price growth to price depreciation, with depreciation rates approaching 10 percent in the West and South.[50]

Among the alarms sounded in the report are the risks posed to buyers and the economy by "adjustable and exotic loans," and by the high debt burdens.[51] The burdens of those loans could prove to be considerable for working Americans when it is considered that housing prices had grown more than twice as fast as income from 1990 to 2005.[52]

Of course the national averages are skewed somewhat by such stratospheric housing markets as Honolulu and San Francisco, where the median price of a house exceeds $600,000 to $700,000, but the overall trends are clear and well documented. In far too many ways, Americans have become overextended with personal debt and are literally banking on the never-ending appreciation of their residences to keep them afloat. In some parts of the country a household's mortgage obligation requires more than one-third of their income – well above historical norms.

In August 2006, USA Today reported that the National Association of Realtors (NAR) had linked the loss of manufacturing jobs to the downward spiral of housing prices in 26 metro areas in second quarter.[53] The portrait painted by the article included that of single parents and other working Americans forced to sell (often at a loss), to refinance or struggle to carry the burden of mortgage debt in a collapsing labor market.

As it became ever clearer in 2005 and 2006 that the entire U.S. economy was over-dependent on the "torrid" housing market, economists and journalists formed a chorus of speculation about when the housing "bubble" might burst or whether American luck and ingenuity could steer this market and the U.S. economy to a soft landing.

Such speculations for the U.S. as a whole are fine as far as they go, but anyone who hopes to have a full understanding of the struggles of America's working class must be fully aware of what is happening *in* the homes and *with* the homes of those who live paycheck to paycheck. All too many have come to realize that neither the family finances nor the U.S. economy can establish firm footing on a bubble of any kind – even a housing bubble made of bricks and mortar.

It is common enough for local media and sometimes national media to provide anecdotal coverage of the issues that confront American workers. Certainly avid news watchers have seen, heard and read dozens or hundreds of stories over the past several years about layoffs in steel, textiles, automobiles and the high-tech industries, in states as diverse as South Carolina, Michigan and Texas.

But one North Carolina study provided an in-depth look at how job dislocations and high unemployment have a widely destructive effect not only on the local economy but on the local social structure and every aspect of a community's well-being.

The Economic and Social Impact of Job Loss in Robeson County, North Carolina 1993 – 2003, by Leslie Hossfeld, Mac Legerton and Gerald Keuster provided a systematic and alarming accounting of what can happen in working class communities when the jobs leave town and the economy goes South.[54]

Robeson County, North Carolina is the most racially diverse rural county in the United States, and it lost almost 9,000 manufacturing jobs from 1993 to 2003.[55] In 1993 manufacturing jobs provided about 31 percent of all the jobs in the county, and in that decade the factory jobs plummeted from 17,430 to 6,832.[56] This resulted in a total regional employment decline of 18,435, and the loss of income across the region reached $674,000 per year by 2004 – a cumulative impact of $808 million.[57]

As a result, by 2004 regional governments were collecting $39 million less in revenues from indirect business taxes, including sales taxes, business taxes and other fees.[58] This does not take into account the loss of income taxes, corporate profits taxes and taxes paid into the Social Security and Medicaid programs. Costs to government unemployment insurance programs nearly doubled from 2000 to 2001, and the growth in the number of workers exhausting their unemployment benefits exceeded 225 percent in one two-year period.[59] Government payments for food stamps, Aid to Families with Dependent Children, energy assistance and other programs shot up by $28 million from 1994 to 2001.[60]

The study revealed that the ripple effects from the lost factory jobs hit local businesses very hard and resulted in significant job losses in businesses as diverse as banking, restaurants, wholesale trade, transportation, the school systems and even the local hospital.[61]

Chronic unemployment became a problem in this rural area, and unemployment rates continued to track at more than double the state level.[62]

Personal bankruptcies in the region quadrupled from 1994 to 2003, increasing steadily from 1999 to 2002.[63] Thirty percent of residents had no access to health insurance, and the infant mortality rate increased from 12.1 percent in 1990 to 14 percent in 2000.[64] This is hardly surprising when both the patients and the hospital workers are losing their jobs as a result of the significant loss in manufacturing jobs.

It is probably fair to characterize as "devastating" the broader economic effects of this working class job loss. What is significant about the trends in Robeson County is the question that must be answered: How many Robeson Counties can be found in the U.S. today?

Danville, Illinois, comes to mind, with its mass layoffs and plummeting housing prices. Any community that has proudly hosted factories owned by General Motors Corporation or Ford Motor Company come to mind. Hundreds of so-called "mill towns" across the Carolinas, and into Alabama and Kentucky can be compared to Robeson County.

And what do these stresses of the social fabric mean behind closed doors, in the living rooms and around the kitchen tables of Middle America?

Johns Hopkins University sociologist Harvey Brenner calculated that for each rise of one percent in the unemployment rate we can expect the following consequences:

- 4 percent more people go to prison;
- 5.7 percent more people are murdered;

- 4.1 percent more people commit suicide;
- 4.3 percent more men and 2.3 percent more women are admitted to mental hospitals; and
- 1.9 percent more people die of heart disease, cirrhosis of the liver and other chronic illness.[65]

The costs to families are significant. Probabilities of separation and divorce increase, and the related stresses contribute to increased incidence of abuse, alcoholism and drug abuse.[66] The links are strong between unemployment and loss of physical and mental health.[67] Children of parents who have lost their jobs may face increased risk of health effects, and at a time when health insurance is either not available or has been dropped because the family can no longer afford it.[68]

Children whose fathers have lost jobs may be more likely to have behavioral and social problems in school, with increased likelihood of suspension, expulsion and the need to repeat a grade.[69] Other studies suggest that academic performance can be lowered overall and that ultimately the child becomes an adult who attains lower occupational status, lower income and greater marital instability.[70]

A University of Michigan study reported that families often must relocate, which disrupts family and support networks, which can further aggravate these family problems.[71] In areas where overall unemployment is high, such as communities that have been affected by large scale manufacturing layoffs, families are driven to rely on public assistance programs and they often fall into a pattern of long-term economic hardship.[72] Single parent families often face more severe economic and emotional hardships as a result of these dislocations.[73]

One report indicated that the "chain of adversity" for families facing unemployment can extend over two years, and the negative effects can linger for the long term.[74] Another study reported that a majority of families with laid off breadwinners had problems paying for basic necessities such as food and clothing, and ended up depleting their savings, if any.[75] Many of these families relied on a variety of methods to get by – everything from visiting emergency food banks to hunting and fishing more to provide food for the table.[76]

One study by Policy Matters Ohio focused on the links between international trade, the loss of blue collar manufacturing jobs, and the economic and social problems confronting workers and their families. The study recapped some existing and familiar findings:

- Manufacturing workers tend to be somewhat older, somewhat less educated, with longer job tenure and tend to have re-employment rates significantly lower than workers from other areas;
- They earned 12 percent less in subsequent jobs than in their previous manufacturing jobs;
- In the areas of the Ohio economy hardest hit by trade-related job losses, the average pay had been more than $17 per hour. In contrast, in those fields with the greatest projected number of job openings, the average pay was less than $10 per hour.[77]

This brings us back to the basic question of the paycheck and the breadwinner's ability to provide for the family. At the very least the breadwinner suffers the loss of self-esteem and confidence that can only come from providing for your family. The picture that emerges of the working class family is one of stresses, dislocations, illness, and a vicious cycle of downward economic and social expectations.

Such portrayals of hardship and struggle may sometimes be at odds with a more general national picture of economic recovery or even good economic health.

How do we reconcile conflicting and contradictory information, which shows that the overall economy is creating new jobs – even if many of those jobs pay less than the ones they replaced? How difficult is it to focus national policy on job losses that are concentrated in only certain economic sectors or Congressional districts when the national unemployment rate is low – even if the unemployment rate is falling because many adults have simply given up and no longer choose to participate in the job market?[78]

The fundamental question may come down to this: In the land of opportunity, how does the working class American see the lay of the land? Does the exploding trade deficit point to a fundamental imbalance in American policies that should support factory jobs and a healthy manufacturing sector? Does the loss of almost 4 million manufacturing jobs that coincides with the surge in our trade deficit spell more trouble than opportunity for the U.S. economy?

And what are the potential connections between these global mega-trends and all those little out-of-the-way mill villages and urban neighborhoods, where factory workers quietly struggle with their diminished expectations, their shrunken paychecks, and the prospects that their families are losing ground that they cannot regain in a lifetime?

Americans value the ideal that prosperity can be achieved by hard working people from any level of society and from any location in the country. We prize our economy's upward mobility. A government that does not share this viewpoint is in danger of alienating the working people who are, indeed, the workhorse of the economy. Neither "protectionists" nor "economic nationalists," America's workers are eager to take on the challenges that accompany a global marketplace, and want leaders in D.C. who will be champions for a level playing field on which American workers can compete.

We are beginning to learn that if we ignore the economic underpinnings of the working class American, we may be undermining the core of our fundamental social contract that has bound us together and enabled us to build the world's greatest economy.

As a cautionary note in this regard, let's consider a recent ill-advised statement from a high-level U.S. government official. In February 2004, in his remarks to the National Economists Club and Society of Government Economists, Dr. N. Gregory Mankiw, Chairman, Council of Economic Advisors, floated this trial balloon:

> This year's report contains a chapter on the challenges facing manufacturing, discussing both the longer term trends and the recent business cycle downturn. There is no question that the recent downturn was particularly hard on manufacturing industries. Manufacturing was affected by the latest economic slowdown

earlier, longer, and harder than other sectors of the economy. We discuss why this has been the case and how the President's policies will help to restore and maintain growth in manufacturing and other job-creating industries.

A box in the Economic Report discusses an important consideration in assessing policies that apply to manufacturing: the definition of what constitutes manufacturing is far from clear. For example, when a fast-food restaurant sells a hamburger, is it providing a service or combining inputs to manufacture a product?

The government agencies that collect data on manufacturing are well aware that the distinction is blurry. According to the Bureau of Labor Statistics, bakeries, candy stores, and custom tailors are all part of manufacturing. But one could walk into such a retailer and see many service activities taking place. Sometimes subtle differences can change how an activity is classified. Mixing water and concentrate to produce a soft drink is classified as manufacturing. If that activity is performed at a snack bar, however, it is considered a service.[79]

Dr. Makiw's somewhat dry and clinical language mirrored that which was also found in the report. Care to guess how such a proposal might be headlined in the media? CBS coverage included this headline: "Building Blue-Collar ... Burgers?"

And here's how the story opened: "Manufacturing jobs making things like airplane engines, cars and farm equipment are disappearing from the American economy. Or are they? According to a White House report, new manufacturing jobs might be as close as your nearest drive-thru. As first reported by The New York Times, the fast food issue is taken up on page 73 of the lengthy government report in a special box headlined, 'What is manufacturing?'"[80]

And what does this media coverage say about the view of things from the perspective of the working class?

Note the fact that the whole concept is buried on page 73 of an obscure report. Note the fact that it was offered in a very matter-of-fact way by some highly respected and learned economists.

Why would the New York Times and CBS News pluck this item from page 73 and run with it? Two possible reasons can be offered. One is that it provided a chance to show how politicians have a "tin ear" when it comes to how the latest government idea might play with working Americans. The second is this: We might not have a formal, lock-tight Webster's dictionary definition for precisely what a manufacturing job is, but as Supreme Court Justice Potter Stewart once said about defining the equally-fuzzy term "obscenity": "I know it when I see it."[81] And "manufacturing" hamburgers is not "it."

The headlines made it clear that there's a certain risk in playing with words when it comes to people's jobs and livelihoods. They also touched a nerve in working class America. If the economy is taking steak off the working man's plate and replacing it with "drive-thru" burgers – manufactured or not – then someone will have to answer for it. And that someone is going to be the disconnected D.C. politicians who refuse to enforce the rules of free trade. Their failures have caused these dramatic negative consequences for working class Americans.

The American voter may be the most intensely surveyed and questioned voter on the face of the earth. Certainly it is difficult to imagine how elections in Japan, Australia or other multi-party democracies could be accompanied by any greater number and variety of polls, surveys, exit polls, opinion polls, marketing surveys, and so forth. And of course the one-party Socialist "peoples' republics" such as China probably don't experience a great compulsion to sample public opinion among their oppressed peasantry – or to respond to it.

But what if – what if we have reached a point in surveying the American electorate where we know more and more about less and less? Or what if we have reached the point where we have so sliced and diced voters by age, race, gender, religion, political party, grandma's ethnicity and other criteria that we have begun to lose focus on something big – something weighty in American politics – something as emblematic of a bygone era as . . . the working class?

Without offering an exact number, most of us would agree that the American working class is big – probably the largest group in the body politic. Blue collar Americans might be seen by some as synonymous with the working class, or making up a significant portion of it. They are millions of people of many races. They are men and women. They are well educated and not well educated. They are native born and immigrant. They are old and young. They are Republican, Democrat, Libertarian, Independent and more.

Michael Zweig, a professor of economics at State University of New York – Stony Brook has broadened the definition and scope of working class and calculated that it makes up as much as 62 percent of the work force – not based on former blue collar-white collar distinctions but based on the worker's place in the pecking order – the amount of power and authority that comes with the job.[82]

For example, Zweig includes such diverse jobs as secretary, bank teller and construction worker, and this can create a broad class of worker that includes white collar work with blue collar sensibilities.[83]

Zweig also notes that the U.S. Department of Labor defines working class as any individual working in a production or non-supervisory capacity.[84]

As David Moberg wrote in *The Progressive* "the old mental image of the working class as made up of blue-collar white guys headed to the factory while their wives and children remain at home is grossly misleading. Women make up nearly half the work force today. Service and office jobs have expanded, and factory work has greatly declined."[85] He also defines "the real swing voter" as "more likely to be a woman who drives an old Chevy Malibu and goes bowling, assuming she can find the time after a hard day as an office worker, airline clerk or nurse's aide."[86]

Might it cloud the issue to expand the working class so as to lose the focus on the blue collar worker? Perhaps; but at the same time, there are issues common across all of working class America that affect the economic well being (and therefore the votes) of the traditional factory workers and their counterparts in other industries and lines of work.

Zweig notes that many American workers identify themselves with the working class, not just based on their current or achieved professional status, but on their class of origin.[87] This is a point on which elected officials should reflect. While outsiders may arbitrarily assign various groups to the working class, the number of people who assign themselves to this group may be larger or more inclusive.

A generation ago, in 1966, Richard F. Hamilton reported that individuals tend to base their present class situation on their class of origin.[88] He indicated that half of all white collar workers at that time considered themselves to be working class.[89]

And if you are a candidate or an interest group seeking to energize a bloc of voters, why not target the largest bloc with the greatest common interests?

Take for example the movement of jobs from the United States to Mexico, China, Korea, Vietnam, or you name it. It is not the investment bankers, executives and others at the top of America's white collar food chain who are losing sleep about the "offshoring" of their jobs (at least not yet. . .). It is the factory workers and the ever widening swath of call center workers, and tech workers.

In a lead up to the 2004 elections, a Harris Interactive survey found that 68 percent of Americans disagreed with the statement that "it is good for the U.S. economy when American companies use less expensive workers in countries like China and India to do work previously done at a higher cost in this country."[90] The movement of American data processing and information technology jobs to India was viewed as negative by 73 percent, and the exporting of call center jobs to India was viewed as negative by 72 percent.[91]

Equally solid majorities disapproved of the export of manufacturing jobs, with 64 percent agreeing that it was a bad idea to use Chinese workers to manufacture goods previously made in the U.S., and 59 percent saying it was a bad idea to use Mexican workers for such manufacturing jobs.[92] These numbers move even closer to 90 percent when Americans learn that many jobs have been transplanted in order to allow companies to take advantage of illegal trade tactics, like currency manipulation.

Almost seven in ten (69 percent) agreed that companies that use less expensive workers to replace American workers should pay a special tax on this work.[93] When these same Americans are educated that the real reasons behind many job losses are illegal and immoral actions, their visceral concerns become deeper and they become more vocal.

When asked in this 2004 survey which Presidential candidate would be likely to have the better policies to deal with these issues, 32 percent indicated John Kerry and 24 percent indicated President Bush.[94] Almost half said "neither" or "not sure" indicating both a problem and an opportunity for Republicans and Democrats at that stage of the campaign.[95]

A study by the Pew Research Center for the People and the Press found similar views by large segments of the electorate coming out of the 2004 elections. Titled, "Beyond Red vs. Blue," the study examined the electorate beyond party affiliations, looked at several key issues, and updated its political "typology" in which several discrete voter groups were identified and described.[96]

With regard to trade and jobs, the study found that 69 percent of Americans considered "outsourcing" to be bad for the country, while just 22 percent considered it good.[97] The report used outsourcing as a label for "the hiring by U.S. businesses of lower-cost workers in other countries to produce goods and services."[98]

It is worthwhile to consider the Pew Center's "typology" as we consider just how broad and deep the category of "working class" might be in the country today, because Pew researchers take their examination of voter attitudes beyond our traditional categories of income and job description.

For purposes of the study Pew determined nine types, three that are primarily Republican, three that are primarily Democrat, and three "middle groups."[99]

The three Republican types are:

- Enterprisers – Staunchly conservative, patriotic, pro-business, and for an assertive foreign policy – tends to be white, educated, affluent, and male;
- Social Conservatives – Tend to agree with Enterprisers but can be critical of business and supportive of regulation to protect the public good and the environment;
- Pro-government Conservatives – Religious, socially conservative but inclined to support relatively more government regulation and policies that assist the poor – a relatively young and female group that tends to be under financial pressure but see it within their power to get ahead.[100]

The three Democrat types are:

- Conservative Democrats – Religious, socially conservative and moderate with regard to foreign policy, and includes blacks, Hispanics and people with a relatively strong sense of personal empowerment;
- Disadvantaged Democrats – Female, poorly educated, least financially secure group that includes a high proportion of minority voters and tend to be distrustful of government and pessimistic about their future;
- Liberals – The largest voting bloc of the Pew typology are affluent, educated, secular, liberal on social issues, oppose assertive foreign policy and strongly support environmental regulation and assistance to the poor.[101]

The three types in the middle are:

- Upbeats – Educated and informed, with positive views of their personal finances, government, business, and the state of the Union – with no formal party affiliation but voted 4-1 for Bush in 2004;
- Disaffecteds – Unsatisfied with their financial situation, cynical about government, less affluent and educated than the Upbeats but strong supporters of aggressive military stance against U.S. adversaries, which in part accounts for a strong leaning toward President Bush;
- Bystanders – As the name implies, this largely younger group do not vote and occupy the political sidelines.[102]

So for the sake of discussion, let's assign the issue of "outsourcing" as a bellwether issue for working class Americans, then look at how these groups view the issue, according to the Pew study.

Look at the large majorities among these groups who view "outsourcing" (as defined above) as bad for the country: Disadvantaged Democrats – 87%; Conservative Democrats – 81%; Disaffecteds – 78%; Pro-Government Conservatives – 71%; and Upbeats – 55%.[103]

That's five of the nine groups with a strong majority opposed to a widespread business practice with demonstrably negative effects on America's working class. It includes solid numbers of voters that identify themselves with both parties and the middle. Significantly, these voters have divergent views on issues ranging from social welfare and foreign policy. In other words, a candidate that took up the gauntlet for this issue, which is critical to the livelihoods of the working class, could reach across all segments of the electorate.

Of interest in the 2006 election season and beyond was the emergence of immigration as a pocketbook issue. Immigration is cast by some as a national security issue insofar as porous borders permit the movement of both illegal aliens and terrorists. But the Pew study determined that opposition to liberal immigration policies such as allowing workers to enter the U.S. to work for a limited period, tends to fall along economic lines rather than the party line.[104]

Almost two thirds of Disadvantaged Democrats (63 percent) opposed easing entry for immigrant workers, with

51 percent of Disaffecteds and 50 percent of both Social Conservatives and Conservative Democrats also opposed to these more permissive immigration policies.[105]

And on the other side of the issue could be found the strange bedfellows of Enterprisers, Liberals and Upbeats, in which solid majorities from 57 percent to 71 percent supported more liberal immigration policies for either philosophical or business reasons.[106]

Studies such as this provide a view of the common concerns of people who don't appear at first to have much in common – at least when measured by the usual categories such as political party, income bracket, gender and race. At the very least, the Pew Research Center provides us with a new Rubik's Cube model of looking at the voters, and as the name of the report implies, if we look beyond red and blue we might turn up a side of the cube with a whole new color – and it just might represent something as big as the working class.

How does one engage the issues of working America? First, let's offer a reminder that it's probably not a good idea to define these voters too narrowly or to get bogged down in a lot of sub-categories based on ancestry, gender and other forms of identity politics. The more inclusively you define voters the more disciplined you can be in charting their common interests and establish their true (or potential) impact on the American political system.

Are elected leaders and policy makers today writing laws and establishing policies as if the lives of Working Class Americans depended on it? Perhaps not, and to be fair, in a time of war and a time of profound disagreement on war, it may be reasonable not to cast blame on certain leaders if they have trouble bringing the working class vote into focus.

On the other hand, a casual tour through the World Wide Web in the months leading up to the 2006 midterm elections revealed an almost fever-pitched lust for all kinds of swing-voter targets. Many groups from the left wing, progressive wing, liberal wing (choose your name) sensed that incumbents and conservatives of various stripes had been put on the ropes by President Bush's commitment to the war in Iraq. Many gleefully put forth the idea that this provided important advantages and momentum to moderate to liberal candidates for the 2006 midterm elections, and then – just as quickly – they advanced the idea that their favorite issue (health care, Medicare, minimum wage, deadline for withdrawal from Iraq, more money for teachers' salaries or whatever) was THE issue to change the balance of power in the U.S. Congress, in governor's mansions and in state legislators.

The great number of voters in America's working class may be excused for thinking that many of these single-issue crusaders may be wide of the target – a charge just as likely to be leveled at pundits on the right wing of the political spectrum.

Contrast the scope of Richard Nixon's "Silent Majority" during the tumultuous Vietnam era with the more focused parsing and paring of the body politic that we see today. Perhaps, in our age, the emergence of "Reagan Democrats" more than 20 years ago launched the idea that each election cycle can bring a discrete bloc of voters that can swing the election and perhaps also exercise the virtue of stumping the pundits.

From Sen. Barry Goldwater's shellacking by President Lyndon Johnson in 1964 to President Reagan's 1980 victory, the conventional wisdom had held that a truly conservative U.S. presidential candidate could not be expected to win a majority of votes. With the so-called Reagan Democrats, that conventional wisdom was jettisoned, and the repercussions are still being felt in electoral politics over two decades later.

The term was essentially launched by an analysis of white, largely union voters in Michigan who had been reliably Democratic in voting for president at one time but who had voted for Reagan in support of issues such as a strong national defense, tax reform and certain social issues. As author of the study, long-time Democrat pollster Stan Greenberg is credited with bringing this group into focus.

One of the reasons that Reagan Democrats (the voters and the concept) captured the imagination of political strategists was because they did not behave as they were supposed to behave. But candidate Reagan demonstrated that working class Americans could no longer be pigeon-holed into certain parties based on any facile assumptions or hoary conventional wisdom.

At the heart of political science we always find the hard work of discovering the obsolescence of our conventional wisdoms. With repetition these truths can become somewhat simple-minded. As Reagan came into his own politically there were many true believers to the effect that union workers voted Democrat and country clubbers voted Republican.

Many continued to hold to this belief even as candidate Reagan became President Reagan by earning the votes of many union members, who had discarded other peoples' conventional wisdom for reasons of their own.

"Reagan Democrats" has probably buttered more bread for more political consultants than could be listed on this page. For example in 1996 "Soccer Moms" became the bonfire around which the D.C. pundits and the candidates danced with enthusiasm and conviction.

"Word Spy" is a clever web site devoted to "lexpionage – the sleuthing of new words and phrases."[107] The posted entry for "Soccer Mom" includes this summary: "Somewhere along the way, the stressed-out, minivan-driving juggler of lives and roles was awarded the title of MVP in the competition for voters. She became the icon of 1996, nearly running over the Angry White Male of 1994 in her new Dodge Caravan."[108]

The site goes on to quote this from a 1996 column by Ellen Goodman: "But in politics, as in soccer, you have to use your head. A trip through the postelection world is a reminder that her role was a touch inflated. Suburban, married moms with kids at home were never more than 6 percent of the voters. Gary Langer at the ABC News Polling Unit calls them simply the 'group du jour.' He fairly sputters at the idea that they could swing anything but a headline."[109]

Goodman's take on this may sound like the last word on the subject, but it wasn't the only word. According to Word Spy, the number of media references for the term "Soccer Mom" skyrocketed from 35 in 1995 to 1,150 in 1996.[110]

For thoughtful candidates, strategists, pundits, and columnists it is of more than passing interest whether you are dealing with the "group du jour" (or as is so often the case of D.C. armchair strategists – the issue de jour) or with something more substantial in the political contest.

Messages are crafted, tested in focus groups, and sharpened to a fine point, all in the hope that some of these various discrete voter groups can be brought over from the other party. There's a raiding party for Soccer Moms or Angry White Males or one of the latest flavors of the month, NASCAR Dads.

NASCAR Dads? By now most people in politics know that this is a catchy name for white males, and heavy on the southern blue collar type. In the run-up to the 2004 elections this group became a hot commodity. Given the devastation in American manufacturing and the loss of millions of the best blue collar jobs in the country, nobody can be faulted for thinking that NASCAR Dads were ripe for the picking.

Journalist Ben Klayman, writing for Reuters in August 2006, opened his story from the Allstate 400 NASCAR race, where he interviewed a 23-year-old white male from Danville, Illinois. (Remember Danville, the city where thousands lost their manufacturing jobs and housing prices collapsed?) The subject of the interview declared himself a "toss-up."[111]

The story reported on a Zogby International poll which found that 56 percent of NASCAR fans believe the U.S. is on the wrong track, and that about equal portions of these voters – approximately a third – planned to vote either Republican or Democrat, leaving another third up in the air.[112]

In past racing seasons and election seasons, Democrat candidates have made some pretty overt attempts to reach these voters. Bob Graham, the U.S. Senator from Florida who ran for the 2004 Democratic presidential nomination, sponsored a vehicle in the NASCAR Craftsman Truck Series. His name spray-painted across the hood of the truck, which provided great name recognition, of course, and clear evidence that "I am one of you" – if by "you" one meant "Sponsor of a NASCAR racing vehicle."

Nonetheless, NASCAR Dads seized the popular imagination (at least among candidates) during the past few years, and so it was duly noted that the President of the United States kicked off the NASCAR season at the Daytona 500 during his 2004 campaign. Not to be outdone, Virginia Governor Mark Warner invested in a stock car team and 2004 Democratic vice presidential candidate, John Edwards, sponsored a race car in Iowa.

The problem with these approaches is that the candidate is trying to build a bridge to this voting bloc by saying, in effect, "I have the same interests that you do!" And while there is some tactical sense in attempting to create similarity between oneself and one's potential constituents, a family that is struggling to make ends meet after the loss of its primary source of income is not going to be overridingly concerned with whether an official likes NASCAR, when he voted for a free trade agreement that led to the local mill closing. It is almost as if political analysts become so caught up in the political monikers that they forget the underlying issues that are common to the group in the first place.

It is this very point that is lost on many of the so-called D.C. experts – or as the current White House prefers, "wedge experts." When the broader issues of family survival and security are placed at risk, the wedge issues fade into relative obscurity in terms of importance to the voters. In other words, for the D.C. pundit to be accurate from 30,000 feet, the variables affecting the electorate have to remain relatively constant from election to election. When issues like personal financial security, which commands broad interest across the electorate, become the focus of an election, the variables change drastically, and the ability to forecast electoral results based on previous data is undermined.

For the women, the latest successor to Soccer Moms is something called "Mortgage Moms." In a September 2006 article, Washington Post writers Jeffrey Birnbaum and Chris Cilliza offered the thesis that midterm election battles might be waged over "square footage and closet space," owing to the economic pressures being brought to bear on families by stagnant wages, volatile energy prices and, now, the potential for interest rate increases to run up the cost of credit card debt and the family home.[113] And, in the spirit of the age, they wrote, "Every election cycle has its own important set of undecided, or swing, voters. In 2000 it was the 'soccer moms,' targeted by both parties with appeals based on education and quality-of-life concerns. In 2003 it was the security moms, normally Democratic-trending women whose concerns about terrorism helped give Bush his margin of victory. This year could mark the emergence of what might be called mortgage moms – voters whose sense of well-being is freighted with anxiety about their families' financial squeeze."[114]

Catchy, isn't it? "Mortgage Moms" has alliteration and requires only two words – just like Soccer Moms, NASCAR Dads, Reagan Democrats and so forth.

It seems to me perhaps the path is too well worn. It is possible that we have reached a point of diminishing returns, where the very definition of political cleverness and astuteness is to define the electorate ever more fine and thin: The smaller the slice the smarter the pundit, pollster or campaign consultant.

"You strain out a gnat and swallow a camel," said Jesus to the Pharisees, when he criticized them for their punctilious observance of the law while missing the law's main point.[115] So those in politics sometimes strain out the gnats of the electorate while swallowing the camels of electoral defeat.

Why? Perhaps we are looking too much at voters under our microscopes. Perhaps they have more in common and see things more in common that we think. Perhaps we ought to reframe them based on fundamental things that they have in common. After all, leaders who believe that the "working class Americans" or the "blue collar Americans" face common issues are bound to be better equipped to address those concerns in order to effect political outcomes.

Just prior to the 2006 midterm elections, we conducted polls in two key Congressional districts: North Carolina's 11th and Indiana's 8th districts (districts which would both change hands on election day). The level of voter education and concern demonstrated by these surveys showed that issues affecting manufacturing were significant issues for the electorate. In a poll of likely voters in both Indiana's 8th and North Carolina's 11th Congressional Districts, 83% and 86%

of likely voters, respectively, considered loss of manufacturing and working class jobs to be important or very important to their vote in the upcoming congressional election.

Were you aware that the U.S. Manufacturing
Sector has lost more than 3 million jobs over the
past several years?

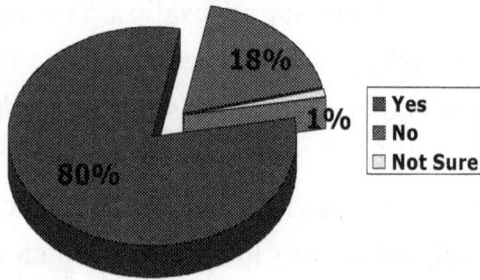

Fig. 3-1 North Carolina's 11th District Survey Results

Voters were very aware that millions of manufacturing jobs
had been lost in recent years - 69% in Indiana and 80% in
North Carolina. Approximately 75% of voters in both districts found the relocation of jobs overseas to be an important or very important issue to their vote, and almost 90% of
voters in both districts said the loss of the jobs was
important to them.

Are the loss of these jobs and un-enforced trade
agreements important to you?

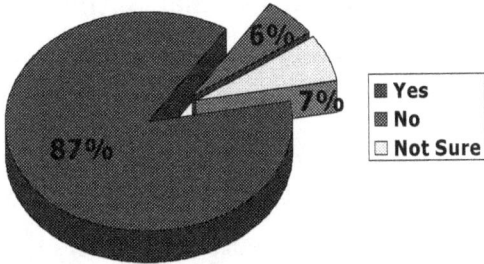

6%

7%

87%

- Yes
- No
- Not Sure

Should the U.S. Congress place a renewed
emphasis on concerns of working Americans?

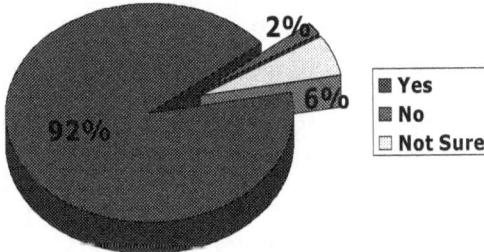

2%

6%

92%

- Yes
- No
- Not Sure

Figs. 3-2 & 3-3 North Carolina's 11th District Survey Results

Over 90% of voters in both districts thought it was critical for Congress to focus on the concerns of working America in the next term. A candidate who spoke to these issues in their campaign would actually be addressing a matter of vital importance to the people in the district. The candidate would show not only that he was similar to the men and women of that district, but that he shared their concern for their ability to provide for their families. Try showing that on the hood of a race car.

In fact, the winning candidates in both of these districts did speak to these issues. Heath Shuler, the Democratic candidate for the 11th District of North Carolina, made sure to point out that his opponent, Republican Charles Taylor, an eight-term incumbent, had done nothing to prevent the hemorrhaging of manufacturing jobs – primarily in the textile industry – from Western North Carolina. Shuler pled his case: "We must end the unfair trade agreements that have cost us our large manufacturing firms, while concentrating on developing new and expanding industries like alternative energy. We must also work diligently to attract smaller and high-tech manufacturing companies."[116] Taylor had already taken a lot of political heat from his constituents for failing to vote against the Central American Free Trade Agreement (CAFTA), and Shuler made sure that every voter in the district knew about it. As one of Shuler's ads stated: "Taylor skipped a critical vote to save thousands of American jobs, but got an award for creating jobs in Russia."[117] Shuler went on to win 54% of the vote, defeating Taylor by over 17,000 votes.

In Indiana's 8th District, Brad Ellsworth, the Democratic challenger, campaigned extensively on the issue of fair trade and jobs for American working families. The Republican incumbent, John Hostettler, focused his campaign on social issues and values, a common strategy among politicians looking to appeal to the "concerns" of the working class voter. Unlike Hostettler, Ellsworth took on the issue of fair trade head-on. The voters responded and handed Ellsworth a decisive victory – a margin of over 45,000 votes and 61% of the vote. Ellsworth acknowledged the importance of the issue in his acceptance speech, stating: "American jobs belong in America and that's where we need to keep them."[118]

Both Shuler and Ellsworth recognized an undercurrent of discontent in their districts, and tapped into it. It is unclear to what extent this issue carried the day for these two Democrats, and I will examine these races and the demographics of their electorate in more detail in Parts 4 and 5 to attempt to provide insight on that question. But I think it is instructive to look at the race in Illinois's 6th Congressional District. Democratic candidate Tammy Duckworth, an Iraq war veteran, ran her campaign on primarily one issue – Iraq, a subject that many pundits have declared the midterm elections to be a referendum upon. And yet Peter Roskam, the Republican candidate, chose to highlight the plight of manufacturing workers in Illinois, stating: "We have a serious problem in Illinois. We lost over 180,000 manufacturing jobs - we can't just let that happen."[119] On a day when Democrats everywhere were swept into office, Roskam captured 51% of the vote, defeating Duckworth by 5,000 votes.

With that in mind, it might give us perspective to ask this question: Can anyone recall or point out a commonly remembered speech by Ronald Reagan that seemed to be crafted to "Reagan Democrats?" Is it likely that he would have bought a race car team in order to embellish his credibility among a slice of a slice of a slice of the voters?

Imagine for a moment these words coming from President Reagan or candidate Reagan: "White folks in the South who drive pickup trucks with Confederate flag decals on the back ought to be voting with us, and not them, because their kids don't have health insurance either, and their kids need better schools too."

Democratic presidential candidate Howard Dean said this, during the same stretch of the campaign it was revealed that he had decided to mention Jesus more in the South than in other regions.[120]

My point in making the contrast is not to denigrate Dr. Dean but to suggest that voters are keenly attuned, consciously or unconsciously, to the contrast. Perhaps working class Americans would have their needs best addressed by being classified in no smaller group than "Working Class America." By doing this, you can make a compelling case to them that there is urgent work to be done on behalf of working men and women – be they Christian or agnostic; people who shoot ducks in the marsh or who just shoot baskets in the gym; and people whose ancestors came from Africa and from Ireland.

Perhaps we reach the point of diminishing returns, when candidates self-consciously style themselves to try to be one of the boys down at the race track (and fail to pull it off

58

because they are arrivistes in suits), or when parties breed ideas that are mutts along the line of "God, Guns and Guts."[121]

This is why candidates often have bags under their eyes. They are up late into the night trying to figure out what in the heck the electorate looks like, which of course can help to explain why they don't always realize what in the heck they themselves look like to the electorate. Perhaps these politicians are spending too much time – and money – trying to manipulate the voters rather than understanding and addressing their concerns. The highest political art is to understand the voters and how they view the world. If a campaigner can get both of these right then it might not be so important whether he rides into town on a rented mule, a stock car, or a golden chariot. See the voters and their landscape as they themselves do, and there will be no need for a wardrobe department.

Jonathan Kaplan wrote this in The Hill in the final weeks of the 2004 election: "But just like other labels, such as 'security moms' – married mothers with children for whom terrorism was a defining issue – and 'office park dads,' NASCAR dads have not materialized as a decisive voting bloc."[122]

The reason for this lack of real voter enthusiasm or turn out stems from trying to energize these voters with contrived special interest sound bites, instead of education on the issues and a display of understanding of the concerns that are meaningful to these voters. And so we must begin to engage voters in a way that acknowledges and respects their most important concerns.

"In towns it is impossible to prevent men from assembling, getting excited together and forming sudden passionate resolves. Towns are like great meeting houses with all the inhabitants as members. In them the people wield immense influence over their magistrates and often carry their desires into execution without intermediaries."

—Alexis de Tocqueville, In Search of Democracy in America

In the fall of 2005, I had the pleasure of addressing over 4,000 people at a town hall in Darlington, South Carolina, on the invitation of Nucor Corporation. An assemblage of concerned citizens, elected officials, and leaders in the manufacturing community gathered together to discuss a range of issues related to the loss of manufacturing jobs in the United States. U.S. Representative John Spratt was in attendance at the event, and U.S. Senator Lindsey Graham prepared a 20-minute video for the audience to explain his support for American manufacturing. Over 100 state and local officials participated. Other national and local manufacturers joined the discussion, such as Bill Hickey, President of Lapham-Hickey Steel, and employees from Chesterfield Lumber Company. The gathering attracted national media attention – CNN's Lou Dobbs had live feed from the event, with Christine Romans reporting. It was an exhilarating experience to be a part of.

I mention this event because I believe the way in which Nucor is taking a leadership role on this issue is a perfect example of how a stakeholder or a candidate can engage voters on issues that matter to them. Let me start by giving some background on what Nucor is doing.

Nucor Corporation is the nation's largest steel producer, with over $14 billion in annual revenues. Processing over 22 million tons of scrap metal every year, Nucor is the world's largest recycler. Nucor employs more than 11,700 employees in 18 states across the nation. Nucor's employees earn an average salary of $70,000 a year. All Nucor employees and their dependents are eligible for a $3,000-per-year scholarship to college or vocational school. I think it is fair to say that Nucor is an excellent example of the type of manufacturing employer any community would be glad to have.

Nucor's chairman, president, and chief executive officer, Dan DiMicco, has taken on the mantle of leadership in the fight to keep American manufacturing jobs in the United States. DiMicco believes that manufacturing can be returned to a position of prominence in the American economy if political action is taken to ensure that existing international trade laws are enforced and domestic laws are reformed to create a level playing field upon which American manufacturers can compete. He has spearheaded the town hall meetings, launched a series of educational forums, engaged the leaders of national manufacturing associations, and even wrote a book on the subject, entitled *Steeling America's*

Future. Nucor has also sponsored a national issue campaign, centered on a web site: America4Sale.net.

The Darlington rally was the ninth in a series of nationwide town hall meetings (and at the time of this writing, two more events had been held), that drew crowds averaging nearly 3,000 people. It's important to note that Nucor engages these communities even in non-election years; Nucor considers it a top priority to educate and energize the people that it needs to run its business in a substantive and non-partisan manner – and who, in return, rely on Nucor for their livelihood.

And Nucor is not the only example of companies and employees standing up for their interests in working class jobs.

- The Metal Services Center Institute (MSCI) is a trade association focused on representing the interests of metal producers, distributors, processors, and users. MSCI has held more than 20 town hall meetings all over the nation since 2003 to discuss the decline of manufacturing in North America, and to propose means to counter this decline.
- Stop Outsourcing Wisconsin was a project of the Wisconsin state AFL-CIO, the Wisconsin Fair Trade Campaign, and Americans for Democratic Action. In 2004, the group held a series of 8 town halls throughout Wisconsin in the months prior to the 2004 elections, urging government to level the playing field for fair and free trade.[123] Similar "Stop Outsourcing our Future" projects were initiated in seven other states.[124]

- On November 2, 2006, six New York manufacturers – Rome Strip Steel, Revere Copper Products, Owl Wire, Diemolding, Varflex, and Kris-Tech Wire – joined up with the Manufacturers Association of Central New York (MACNY) to hold a town hall meeting "to generate awareness and action to level the playing field and halt the unfair and illegal trade practices of foreign governments and to garner support for key federal and state tax and regulatory changes critical to the manufacturing sector."[125] MACNY claims as members more than 300 manufacturing companies, who provide jobs for over 55,000 people in nineteen counties throughout Central New York.[126]

Now conventional wisdom would say that it is hard to engage voters on such obscure issues as currency manipulation, trade law enforcement and other underlying causes of job loss. But when you see traffic backed up for a mile or more as people turn out, even when the weather is cold or rainy, you know that there are great underlying concerns in America's working class, and that people can still be awakened and roused to action.

Another voice beginning to weigh in on the erosion of the standard of living for America's working class is coming from the pulpits and lecterns of America's spiritual leaders. As town hall meetings on behalf of American manufacturing have spread across the country, there is a growing interest from pastors and congregations to become involved on behalf of working class citizens.

Voters in Rust Belt states and others where good jobs have been replaced by not-so-good jobs or long-term unemployment have been brought home to the fact that much of the Christian gospel is directed to people who are disadvantaged by poverty, sickness and lack of social standing.

It is said that there are 3,000 verses in the Bible that deal with the poor, and when Evangelicals decide to get focused on the economy, their elected leaders should not fail to take note. The Barna Research Group reports that 89 percent of Evangelicals are registered to vote. CNN exit polling of voters in the 2006 House of Representative races recorded that 34 percent of voters identified themselves as "evangelicals." Clearly this is an active and influential voting group.

The Associated Baptist Press reported recently that surveys among Christian voters have shown an increase in concern about poverty and joblessness, which may not be surprising in light of the well-documented erosion in job security among virtually every class of worker, along with the erosion of earning power experienced by many members of the working class.

Diverse think tanks and interest groups are emerging to give voice and shape to this intersection of faith and civic interest. For example, Call to Renewal bills itself as a faith-based movement to overcome poverty. The Acton Institute has been described as more "laissez-faire" organization that deals with economic and social issues. Other evangelical leaders are speaking up in key battleground states.

We Believe Ohio is a group of more than 300 clergy from across Ohio that has decided to speak up on the effects of offshoring on the American working class. Formed in 2005, We Believe Ohio is made up of "pastors, priests, rabbis, cantors, and actively committed lay leaders from Roman Catholicism, two traditions of Judaism, and over fifteen Protestant denominations." They are committed to "informing and engaging members in the electoral process" with the goal of achieving 80 percent of member turnout. Reverend Sydney Jackson explained, "People talk about Jesus' views on sexuality. . . but more central to the matter of piety is how we treat the least among us. . . . 'Oppressing the poor in order to enrich oneself, and giving to the rich, will lead only to loss.' You are not to take advantage of the poor by illegal or legal means, 'for the Lord pleads their case and despoils the life of those who despoil them' (Prov. 22:23)."

Another We Believe Ohio member, Reverend Marvin McMickle of Antioch Baptist Church critiqued legislators who only spoke to Christians about issues like gay marriage and abortion. ""They never discussed . . . that 45 million Americans have no health insurance, [or] the staggering rate of unemployment driven by outsourcing of jobs and downsizing."[127]

Based on my experience in recent years at the grassroots, it is reasonable to assert that the social, religious and economic links between evangelicals and working class voters are there to be made and to be made stronger. The message coming from these religious leaders and their congregations to the politicians in D.C. is: "I know your deeds, that you are neither cold nor hot. I wish you were either one or the other! So, because you are lukewarm—neither hot nor cold—I am about to spit you out of my mouth."[128]

It's clear to me that a these voters are just waiting to be engaged in a substantive way on the issues that affect their lives. Let's take a closer look at the how's and why's.

With such an evenly divided electorate and such volatile issues, America's political parties and candidates should see opportunity – or should brace for an earthquake. The 2006 political atmosphere was charged with anticipation of big gains for the Democrats, and Republican fervor to hold the fort.

The question is: just how far did this charged atmosphere and anticipation extend among the ranks of everyday voters?

Although the political landscape in America was and is primed to be shaken along the fault lines of prosperity and hardship, or war and peace, many of voters are often otherwise engaged.

The Joan Shorenstein Center on the Press, Politics & Public Policy at Harvard University's John F. Kennedy School of Government conducted what it characterized as "the most exhaustive study yet of citizen involvement in an election campaign" during the 2000 election. The findings of that study were reported in a book titled, "The Vanishing Voter: Civic Involvement in an Age of Uncertainty," written by Thomas E. Patterson.

Among the findings highlighted by the Shorenstein Center are:

- Weakening of American political parties as objects of thought and loyalty has reduced the incentive to participate, <u>particularly among lower-income Americans</u> (emphasis mine);

- Modern campaign techniques turn off citizens – even those who are interested in public affairs;
- Attack journalism has corroded Americans' trust and interest in partisan politics, and especially among young adults;
- Americans today think about – and talk about campaigns less than previous generations, and one cited cause is the ever growing volume of so-called soft news; and
- In a related development, network cutbacks on election telecasts have reduced the opportunities for Americans to inadvertently tune in and gain access to campaign and election coverage and events.[129]

As an example, the report cites the fact that 60 percent of American households tuned in to watch the 1960 presidential debate between Sen. John Kennedy and Vice President Richard Nixon, but in 2000 less than 30 percent of households tuned in to the debates between Governor George Bush and Vice President Al Gore.[130]

The report delivers the unsettling news that the period 1960 to 2000 "marks the longest ebb in voter turnout in the nation's history."[131]

Perhaps the glib, tossed-off sound bites about how bad "partisan politics" has been for America obscure the possibility that partisan politics, if done right, can strengthen political parties, which in turn can bring people into the political process at the grass roots level.

But then perhaps we should not be surprised that in an age when every candidate seems to be groomed and prepped for talking to the television cameras that the more traditional arts of talking to the people and organizing political parties have been discarded or degraded from lack of proper use. If the grass is always greener in the mass media, the grassroots may suffer from neglect.

In 2004 the United States saw an uptick in voter participation. The percent of eligible voters who voted in that election reached 64 percent, up from 60 percent in 2000.[132] 89 percent of registered voters voted, up from 86 percent.[133] Fifteen million more people voted, while the voting age population increased by 11 million.[134]

Meanwhile, working class Americans, if you generally consider those to have somewhat less income and education than their white collar counterparts, are leaving a portion of their ballot-box power at home. They are not turning out to vote at the same rate as those people with higher family incomes and educational attainment.

For political candidates or officeholders who craft policies for these voters and desire their votes, this may be seen as a problem – but it also provides a tremendous opportunity. The Census Bureau reports that less than 40 percent of eligible citizens with less than a high school education voted in 2004.[135] About 56 percent of those with a high school diploma or GED equivalent turned out to vote, compared to about 78 percent of people with a bachelor's degree and 84 percent of those with advanced degrees.[136] The largest group in this breakdown, at almost 39 million people, includes those with some college or an associate's degree, and about 69 percent of these people voted in 2004.[137]

People with family income of less than $20,000 had the lowest voting rate of all income groups, and as incomes rose so did so did voting rates, as follows:

- Less than $20,000: 48%
- $20,000 - $29,999: 58%
- $30,000 - $39,999: 62%
- $40,000 - $49,999: 69%
- $50,000 - $74,999: 72%
- $75,000 - $99,999: 78%
- $100,000 and over: 81% [138]

Almost a third of non-voters (30%) in 2004 came from the $20,000 to $49,999 income bracket, yet this group represented the second largest group of potential voters, at 27.3 million people, exceeded only by the 31 million people in the $50,000 to $99,999 income bracket.[139] As these voters are energized, over 8 million new ballots will be delivered, nationwide. Through education regarding real solutions to the problems that matter most to them, these voters will begin to reengage the system. And this is exactly what began to occur in 2006.

People generally state several reasons why they don't vote. The most common reason (20% of voters) is that voters are too busy, or have conflicting work or school schedules.[140] Fifteen percent fail to vote because they are sick, disabled or have family emergencies (and this group was proportionally high among older citizens).[141] Only 11 percent of voters are not interested or believe their vote makes no difference.[142] Ten percent of voters don't like any of the candidates, or the issues they are promoting.[143]

Clearly there are some inroads to be made not only among working class voters, but also among working class citizens who cannot summon the motivation to overcome schedules, indifference or disillusionment in order to vote.

As the "political" issues become more personal, these voters will become more motivated. (One might suggest that the reason that 81% of the highest income voters turn out is to protect their personal interests.) Education of the working class on issues that directly affect their lives will increase their desire to participate in the electoral system, and cause a shift in the existing political paradigm.

Where does this leave the incumbents and the challengers and the consultants and the rest of us as we try to understand what is happening with working Americans and how this could be brought to bear in elections?

The orthodox channels of communications and the predictable political mantras about war and peace, haves and have-nots, do not seem to constitute an effective and coherent communication to the working class. And we've already been given a clue that such self-conscious stunts as posing down at the NASCAR track might just fall wide of the mark.

Remember the one-third of non-voters who were "too busy" or had schedule conflicts that prevented them from voting? That's probably the reason that most of us would cite for not making time for a variety of "chores."

Is voting a "chore?" Is getting involved in the crucial issues of the day a "chore?"

Maybe. But the key is to make sure working class voters know that their vote is critical to the continuity of their way of life.

Abraham Maslow was an American psychologist, who in 1943 proposed a Hierarchy of Human Needs, which he and others continually revised in the following decades.[144] The general premise of Maslow's theory is that a person must fulfill certain basic needs before she is able to focus on other needs. For example, there is an innate drive in human beings to secure basic physiological needs, such as food and sleep. When those needs are not being met, it is difficult – if not impossible – for a person to concentrate on other less basic concerns.

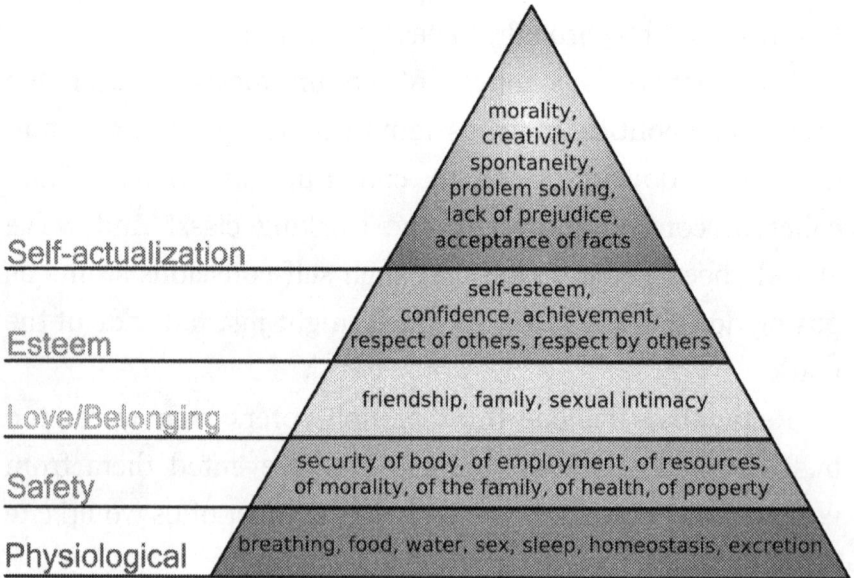

Fig. 4-1 Maslow's Hierarchy of Human Needs[145]

The same analysis applies to each level of the pyramid. If a person's job security is threatened; if their ability to provide for their family, to stay in their house, to pay their medical bills are not certain; then that person will have a difficult time caring about more ethereal issues like corruption in government and the morality of the society in which they live.

Therefore, our thinking should turn to the fundamental questions from the perspective of the voters (and non-voters, for that matter):

- Can I provide for myself and my family?
- Can I get/keep a decent job?
- Can I get medical treatment and care to maintain my health and that of my family?
- Can I work with my employer and my government to set aside money for old age and disability?

Is it really as simple as food, shelter, medical care and old age? Maybe when times are good we can come up with longer political wish lists, but for people who live paycheck to paycheck, such questions are the stuff of which real life is made. They are the basis for the enlightened self-interest that is so fundamental to a working democracy, and these are the broader concerns of the body politic.

Consider this: In 2006, we researched voter concerns in nine states as diverse as Alabama, Illinois and New York, and we asked voters if they were concerned about a major wage earning in their family losing a job.

This is one of those gut-level, baseline worries in life, and it either dogs you or it doesn't. In those nine states, from mid-2004 through mid-2006 we measured a significant level

73

of job insecurity among average Americans. The lowest level we measured was in South Carolina in 2005, where 29 percent of voters indicated they were worried about the loss of a job in their family. We measured the highest level of worry among Indiana voters in 2004, at 46 percent.

The average for the nine states was 40 percent. This is a significant level of worry – focused on one of the most fundamental necessities in life. But it probably explains many things – and answers such diverse questions as, "Why would 4,000 people turn out for a town hall meeting on lost manufacturing jobs?" and "Why are voters expressing such a high level of disenchantment with elected officials, up to and including the U.S. Congress?"

One problem with worry, of course, is that it sometimes lacks focus. People "worry" about the weather, but that doesn't necessarily mean they are going to start riding a bicycle to work to stave off global warming.

After being told that a lot of people are worried about their jobs, it is a fair enough question to ask: "So what?"

Let me ask you a question in return: do you want to do something about it? Do you want to harness the energy from that worry and use it to get elected to office? Do you want to harness the negative energy and use it to work against someone's reelection? Does the worry get focused into an issue or does it just remain a useless force, exerting drag and friction on the body politic, on the economy and on our quality of life?

In surveying the landscape from the working class perspective it is good to remind ourselves that our states, Congressional districts, and even our towns and cities have diverse political and social landscapes. Effective political practitioners use the "lay of the land" to their advantage every day.

Consider this mid-year 2006 WNBC/Marist Poll of registered voters in New York State: When voters were asked to identify the "top priority for the next governor" the answers helped bring the voters and their landscapes into focus.

Twenty-nine percent of New York City voters said that education should be the top priority.[146] In contrast, voters from Upstate New York, which has been hit hard by manufacturing layoffs and a stagnant economy, ranked education fourth – far behind taxes (28 percent) and jobs (21 percent).[147] By comparison, only 11 percent of New York City voters thought that the governor's top priority should be jobs.[148] The third-ranking concern of Upstate voters was economic development, which is basically another way of saying "jobs."[149]

As a result, almost half of these Upstate voters, 41 percent, placed jobs and economic development at the top of the new governor's priorities.[150] That was nearly twice the percentage of voters in New York City that named those as the priority issues; for them it was education and protection from terrorism – the latter not surprising in light of September 11, 2001.[151]

And of course we see this across almost every state in the Union. We see regions of prosperity alongside struggling local economies. International bankers fly out of airports in U.S. financial centers, gazing out of the airliner's widows at shuttered factories or steel mills as the plane ascends to cruising altitude.

If you're a New South Banker working out of Charlotte or Atlanta on global transactions, your home state might appear quite different than if you were laid off from a textile mill or furniture factory and you have spent the past three years struggling to find a reliable job with a good wage and benefits package.

Mortgage lenders in new office parks in Indiana may look at the same landscape as a former steel worker or auto worker, but because they have participated in the boom market for housing, they may not see the same social or political landscape as many of their fellow Hoosiers.

And from such disparities our nation's political architecture presents us with contrasts, conflicts and opportunities. Even as we widen our scope to encompass the entire working class, we can sharpen our focus to see and understand where they live and how they view their social and political landscape.

Take for example Georgia's 12th Congressional District. It stretches from deep in the Piedmont, down along the Savannah River to the coastal port city of Savannah. This district provides a good example of a political landscape in which the working class can make a difference in the outcome of an election – and in which party has the majority in the U.S. House of Representatives.

In 2004, Republican Representative Max Burns lost the election with 48.2 percent of the vote to Democrat John Barrow, who captured 51.8 percent. This was just two years after Burns had won the seat for the first time with 55.2

percent. Two years after his defeat, Burns once again captured his party's nomination and set out to win back the seat.

This made the working class voters of cities such as Savannah, Augusta and Statesboro critically important to the national balance of power, and by virtue of this importance, to the national political agenda for working men and women.

But the towns of Wren, Wadley, Millen, Louisville, and Waynesboro are equally important because they are home to the district's leading manufacturers.

In 2000, the majority of voters in this district voted for Al Gore. In 2002 the majority voted for the Republican nominee for the U.S. House of Representatives. In 2004, the majority voted for the Democrat House nominee and Democrat Presidential nominee John Kerry.

By the 2006 election, the college town of Athens had been moved out of the 12th district through the state legislature's redistricting. Various arguments can be made regarding the potential advantage this gives to Republican candidates, but the solid, unassailable fact remains: the 800-pound electoral gorilla in the room remains the working class voters of the district.

About 70 percent of the households in the district have incomes less than $50,000, and just a fraction less than 64 percent of families earn less than this benchmark amount. The 2005 median family income was $43,864 for the 12th district, well below the national average of $55,832.[152]

Consider, too, the rural character of many communities in this district and the fact that in nearly one quarter of rural U.S. counties, personal income did not keep pace with inflation, due in part to the loss of manufacturing jobs, on which rural counties were particularly dependent to maintain wages and the local standard of living.[153]

But there is more to this district than just electoral volatility and lower-than-average incomes. My team and I conducted an analysis of this and 13 similar Congressional districts in 2006, focusing on a number of variables that we believe can identify certain districts as "fault lines" for shifts in the political landscape – district-level political "earthquakes" if you will.

We developed a tool to help quantify the importance and potential impact of working class voters on any election. We focused on manufacturing workers, because of their pivotal place in recent employment and economic trends and their status as a discreet group.

The heart of our quantitative approach is a Domestic Manufacturing Quotient (DMQ), which is the ratio of the number of expected voters in an electoral region that have a direct stake in a manufacturing job relative to the number of votes by which the last election was decided.

If a Congressional or legislative district includes a critical mass of voters who consist of manufacturing employees and their families, one can expect that working class issues in general, and certain manufacturing issues in particular, can play a significant factor in the district's vote.

North Carolina's 11th Congressional District serves as a good example. In 2002 (I'm referring to the last midterm election because there tends to be significantly higher turnout in Presidential election years, so one must make sure not to compare apples and oranges), Representative Charles Taylor won by a total of 25,671 votes – a thirteen percent margin of victory (56% to 43%). For a candidate looking to secure electoral victory over Taylor, it would not be necessary to change the minds of all 25,671 voters. If just over half that total – 12,836 voters – decide to cast a different vote, Representative Taylor's opponent would have been elected.

In the 2005 American Community Survey, the U.S. Census Bureau estimated that 39,877 people were employed in manufacturing in the 11th District. If we assume that every manufacturing job supports 1.7 voters (employees and spouse or voting-age dependent), then we can calculate that North Carolina's 11th District has 67,790 eligible voters who directly depend on the future of manufacturing in their district.

It is noteworthy that in this district, the census indicates that 15,416 workers have lost their jobs in manufacturing since the 2000 census. Using the same 1.7 multiplier, this adds another 26,207 voters who have reason to focus on the candidates' positions on manufacturing issues. However, for the purposes of this example, let's conservatively focus on those voters with a current and direct stake in manufacturing.

The 11th District had a voter registration rate in 2006 of approximately 97 percent. Therefore, we can assume that 65,757 registered voters will be directly affected by the manufacturing economy and have a direct stake in its health.

Using this figure in the Domestic Manufacturing Quotient formula, we get the following result:

Manufacturing Voters / Δ of last election = DMQ
65,757 / 25,671 = 2.56 = DMQ

In other words, these "manufacturing voters" account for twice the difference between the incumbent and his opponent in the 2002 election, and more than <u>four</u> <u>times</u> the number of votes needed to change the outcome of that election.

The influence of manufacturing issues in elections can be broadened by taking into account manufacturing's strong multiplier effects throughout an area's economy. One rule of thumb holds that for each manufacturing job in a region, four additional jobs are created and supported.[154]

Based on this we can calculate what is termed a Broader Manufacturing Quotient (BMQ). This brings into the equation voters whose economic livelihoods and well-being are linked through direct spending of the high manufacturing wages with local retail merchants, the increased taxes off of the high manufacturing payrolls to pay for government employees such as teachers, and through supplies and raw materials purchased through local vendors and suppliers.

All of these merchants, suppliers, vendors and public sector employees are also voters who can be made aware of how their economic well-being is linked to that of local manufacturing. So the BMQ enables us to broaden the political scope and while focusing the message on a much more diverse electorate than just factory workers – even while showing the broader community's stake in the continued strength of the local manufacturing base.

Returning to our example of the North Carolina 11th Congressional District, this widens the political playing field to encompass approximately 159,508 eligible voters, or

151,532 registered voters who make up the broader manufacturing voters.

Broader Manufacturing Voters / Δ of last election = BMQ
$151,532 / 28,521 = 5.31 = BMQ$

In other words, these manufacturing voters account for five times the difference between the incumbent and his opponent in the 2004 election, and more than <u>ten times</u> the number of votes needed to change the outcome of that election. Given that only 290,897 people voted in the 2004 election, the broader manufacturing voters have the potential to account for more than 50% of the vote in the district.

As I mentioned in Part 3, the Democratic candidate in the 2006 election, Heath Shuler, hammered Representative Taylor for his failure to vote against CAFTA, and spoke repeatedly about protecting the jobs of manufacturing workers in Western North Carolina. Shuler captured 54 percent of the vote, to Taylor's 46 percent, defeating the incumbent by just over 17,000 votes. In fact, Shuler was only one of two Democratic candidates for Congress in 10 southern states that was able to defeat a Republican incumbent.[155]

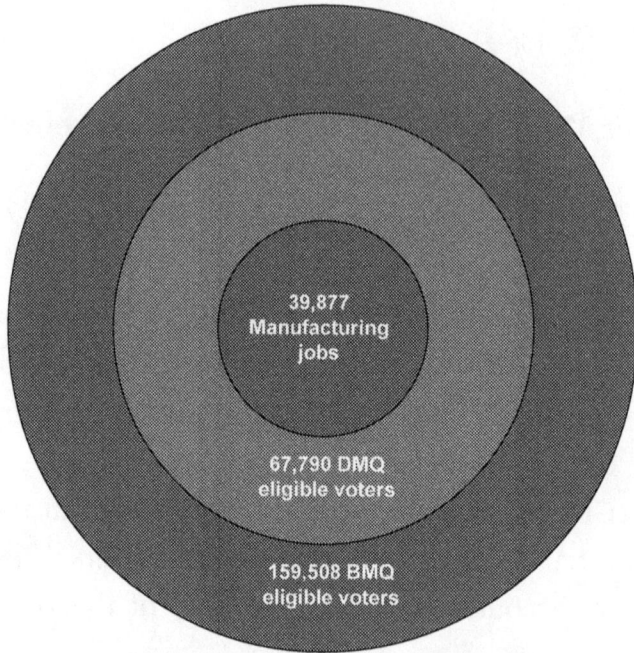

2002: Rep. Taylor won by 25,671 votes

Fig. 4-2 Votes Tied to Manufacturing in NC-11

If we look back to the previous midterm election in 2002, Taylor had won that race by 25,671 votes. From the perspective of the D.C. pundits, who assume that all the variables have remained the same, one might begin looking for where these votes went. Yet something else happened in 2006. Voter turnout increased almost 15 percent from 2002 to 2006 – some 28,500 votes; more than enough to shift the balance of this election. Something overcame all those excuses that voters typically have and made this election a "chore" they believed was worth performing.

The point I'm trying to make is this: in a district like North Carolina's 11th district, an informed and activated manufacturing electorate has the potential to deliver more than 65,000 votes to one candidate or the other, easily making the difference in this race.

And it's clear that the electorate in this district was informed and activated. Shortly before the 2006 midterm elections, we conducted a poll of 400 registered voters in North Carolina's 11th Congressional District. 40 percent of the respondents identified themselves as Republican, with Democrats and Independents accounting for 28 and 27 percent, respectively. Over 50 percent of respondents' household income was no more than $49,000 – note that the national median household income was $46,326. Nine percent of these voters were unemployed. Full-time jobs were held by 49 percent, and 8 percent had part-time jobs.[156] 25 percent of them had experienced some sort of job loss in their family since 2000, and in half of those cases, the layoff had had caused serious or very serious economic harm to their families. Almost 60 percent of these individuals believed that American workers, in general, were in a weaker job and financial situation than in 2002 – only 14 percent believed the situation had improved! With the experience and perspective of these voters in mind, what follows is what they told us about the issues that matter to them.

An amazing 80 percent of voters indicated they were aware that U.S. manufacturing had lost over 3 million jobs over the past several years. 87 percent stated that the loss of these jobs and failure to enforce trade agreements were important to them. When asked if Congress should place a renewed emphasis on the concerns of working Americans, 92 percent said "Yes." And yet less than 20 percent of those same voters believed that Congress would take any such action. That is a sad indictment of our elected officials in Washington, D.C. These voters are just waiting for a candidate – and a Congress – that will prove them wrong.

When we asked these North Carolina voters to what extent a number of issues were important or very important to determining their vote, they responded:

- Medicare / Social Security – 88%
- Loss of Manufacturing Jobs – 86%
- Price of Gasoline – 82%
- Relocation of Jobs to Other Countries – 77%
- Personal or Family Financial Situation – 73%
- Central American Free Trade Agreement (CAFTA) – 53%

Clearly, the voters were aware of and concerned about issues that affected their wallets and pocketbooks – their ability to provide for their families.

And so how did this awareness and concern manifest itself? Aside from the direct effect on the ballots, a fourth of voters indicated they had participated in some sort of grassroots political activity leading up to the 2006 elections. Executives and managers from local manufacturers mailed letters to the candidates urging action on issues that affect their ability to keep jobs in the state. Local officials in Polk, Yancey, Graham, Clay, and Cherokee counties memorialized their strong concern and support for manufacturing in their counties, cities, and towns, by urging their delegations to the state legislature and Congress to take a stand for trade policies that promote fair trade and competition. Although we don't have specific exit polls for the district, voters across the nation placed the economy among the top three causes of concern and reasons for voting among voters; 39 percent of voters said the economy was an extremely important factor in their vote. Iraq did not make the top three.

Now obviously, political strategists and candidates have been looking at districts such as North Carolina's 11th and Georgia's 12th Congressional Districts as political battlegrounds, but I contend that they have underestimated the effectiveness of mobilizing the working class voters and failed to grasp the perspective these voters have of the political landscape. Along with the specific quantitative measures I outlined above, broader employment trends, income trends, factory closings, political volatility, demographic profiles and many other factors can be woven together to portray districts that may be primed for a political temblor.

Remember we cited earlier the lower registration and voting rates among voters of certain income brackets, and we cited some reasons offered for voter disengagement from the electoral process. If districts such as the 12th Congressional District of Georgia are to be targeted and won by candidates of either party – or if stakeholders in those districts want to ensure that their representative is responsive to their needs – potential success lies in formulating platforms and messages that relate to the experience of people who work very hard for less than average money, people who have struggled to maintain full employment in a globalizing economy, people who have struggled to educate their children, fuel their vehicles, purchase medical care, and save for their old age on flat or declining wages.

A question such as this could be posed to a candidate: What would happen in districts such as Georgia's 12th District if you spoke seriously and in depth to working class voters, proposing policies to:

--*enhance* their standard of living and economic security;

--*preserve* or enhance their jobs and job prospects;

--*reform* our current systems of taxation and medical insurance; and

--*bring* the focus of our elected leaders back to the working class?

Let's consider Indiana. Early in the game, our research indicated that forces in Indiana might be building deep underground – setting the stage for the earth to move in three Congressional districts: the 2nd, the 8th and the 9th.

Again, you are looking at districts where in no case does the median family income exceed $51,000 – or between $6,000 and $7,000 below the national median family income.157 And the median household income in Indiana fell almost five percent from 2000 to 2005.

The Indiana Institute for Working Families, in its 2005 report, "The Status of Working Families in Indiana," revealed some of the underlying economic and social pressures that made these three districts subject to some political ground-shaking:

- Indiana lost over 96,000 manufacturing jobs from 2000 to 2006; and it added only 71,000 jobs in the service sectors that showed some strength during the period – leisure and hospitality, professional and business services, and health and educational services.

- Indiana wages fell to 90 percent of the U.S. average over the past several years as a result of the statewide and nationwide erosion of the manufacturing base. The average earnings in manufacturing were $66,300 compared with $34,080 for all jobs.

- The "increasing dominance of service sector industries" in the Indiana economy led to a lack of high-wage jobs in the state.

- Another likely casualty of the manufacturing job loss was the loss of health insurance coverage reported by the ICHHI, which declined from 64.2 percent covered in 1998-2000 to 57.7 percent covered in 2003-2005, and the percent of children covered by private sector insurance declined from 79.5 percent to 67.6 percent in during this period.

- Union participation declined from 16.2 percent of workers in 1998 to 12.4 percent in 2005.[158]

What's interesting is how closely the opinions of the voters in Indiana's 8th Congressional District mirrored their counterparts in Western North Carolina. We conducted an identical poll of 400 registered voters in Indiana's 8th District. 42 percent of the respondents identified themselves as Republican, with Democrats and Independents accounting for 27 and 26 percent, respectively. Forty-eight percent of respondents' household income was no more than $49,000. Eight percent of these voters were unemployed. Full-time jobs were held by 48 percent, and 12 percent had part-time jobs.[159] Twenty-eight percent of them had experienced some sort of direct job loss in their family since 2000, and in 64 percent of those cases, the layoff had had caused serious or very serious economic harm to their families. Over 60 percent of these individuals believed that American workers, in general, were in a weaker job and financial situation than in 2002 – only 11 percent believed the situation had improved! Again, now that we have some grasp of experience and perspective of these voters in mind, we turn to what they told us about the issues that matter to them.

Just under 70 percent of voters indicated they were aware that U.S. manufacturing had lost over 3 million jobs over the past several years. Eighty-eight percent stated that the loss of these jobs and failure to enforce trade agreements were important to them. When asked if Congress should place a renewed emphasis on the concerns of working Americans, 93 percent said "Yes." And yet only 21 percent of those same voters believed that Congress would take any such action. Again, the Indiana voters have no more faith in Congress than those voters in North Carolina.

When we asked the Indiana voters to what extent a number of issues were important or very important to determining their vote, they responded:

- Medicare / Social Security – 87%
- Loss of Manufacturing Jobs – 83%
- Personal or Family Financial Situation – 81%
- Price of Gasoline – 76%
- Relocation of Jobs to Other Countries – 78%
- Central American Free Trade Agreement (CAFTA) – 49%

When we compare these results with the answers we received in North Carolina, what do we learn? Well, one thing is clear: working class issues resonate in both Appalachia and the Rust Belt. And I guarantee these are not the only regions of the country where this bell is being heard.

In recent years, Indiana has led the United States in the portion of its work force engaged in manufacturing, and it continues to be a manufacturing powerhouse. But as in other states, such as North Carolina, New York, and neighboring Illinois, it is losing ground to floods of imports from unfairly competing foreign countries and the large scale relocation of jobs to Latin America and Asia. To add insult to injury, Indiana manufacturers, like their counterparts around the U.S., must compete under the burdens of unnecessarily high energy costs and regulatory frameworks that hamper their competitiveness. In other words, some of the damage to U.S. workers is self-inflicted.

As the nation entered the fall election season for the 2006 mid-term elections, Indiana's manufacturing sector was still more than 99,000 jobs below the 1999 peak employment.

As we focused our research on Indiana's 2nd, 8th, and 9th districts, we concluded that the close margins of recent elections and electoral volatility would make compelling reasons to draw a direct connection between the working class voter and the outcome of local, state and federal elections.

Let's look more closely at Indiana's 8th Congressional District. In 2002, Representative John Hostettler won by approximately 10,000 votes. In the 2005 American Community Survey, the U.S. Census Bureau estimated that 59,475 people were employed in manufacturing in the 8th District. If we assume that every manufacturing job supports 1.7 voters (employees and spouse or voting-age dependent), then we can calculate that Indiana's 8th District has 101,107 eligible voters who directly depend on the future of manufacturing in their district.

The 8th District has a registration rate of 96.5 percent. Therefore, we can assume that 97,568 registered voters will be directly affected by the manufacturing economy and have a direct stake in its health.

Using this figure in the Domestic Manufacturing Quotient formula, we get the following result:

$$\textbf{Manufacturing Voters} / \Delta \textbf{ of last election = DMQ}$$
$$\textbf{97,568 / 10,000 = 9.76 = DMQ}$$

In other words, these "manufacturing voters" account for almost 10 times the difference between the incumbent and his opponent in the 2002 election, and almost <u>20 times</u> the number of votes needed to change the outcome of that election.

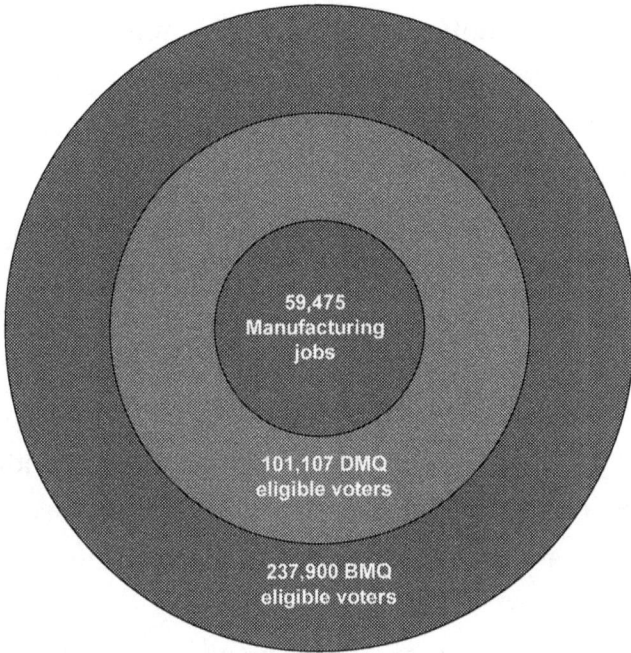

2002: Rep. Hostettler won by 10,000 votes

Fig. 4-3 Votes Tied to Manufacturing in IN-8

As I mentioned in Part 3, the Democratic candidate in the 2006 election, Brad Ellsworth, criticized Representative Hostettler's failure to address the needs of manufacturing workers, and spoke repeatedly about protecting the jobs of manufacturing workers in Indiana. Ellsworth railed, "Today, our economy is shaky at best. Too many jobs are being shipped overseas while wages for the jobs left here at home are stagnant." Hostettler campaigned on social conservative values. Again, paraphrasing Maslow: the first priority for people is the security of their jobs, their homes, and their families. Values are something you worry about after you know you are secure. Ellsworth preached that he knew it was getting harder and harder for working families in Indiana to make ends meet. And Ellsworth captured 61 percent of the vote, to Hostettler's 46 percent, crushing the incumbent by over 46,000 votes.

Again, there was an noticeable increase in voter turnout in 2006. Turnout increased almost 10 percent from 2002 to 2006 – some 20,000 votes. I'll reiterate the point I made a few moments ago: an informed and activated manufacturing electorate in Indiana's 8th Congressional District has the potential to deliver almost 100,000 votes to one candidate or the other, either by activating voters who previously stayed home, or by shifting voter choice to a candidate who speaks to the issues most critical to them.

Imagine – just for the sake of creating a mental picture – that you are a factory worker, or married to a factory worker.

Now imagine that you or your spouse has lost a job. Your plant closed and scores of people with an average tenure of 18 years lost their jobs. But it wasn't a huge factory, and your company wasn't a big name company, therefore the story was buried on the third page of the business section and was bumped on the local television newscast by a spectacular pile-up on the bypass.

The world, the nation, your state, your county, your news media – hardly any of them paused more than a moment during the busy day to consider what happened to your job loss and its potential impacts on you or the nation.

Imagine that you were out of work for nine months, after which you had a bundle of debts and a new job paying just a little more than half what you previously were paid – while your insurance premium more than doubled – and with no pension.

Now imagine that your old job was moved to China. Although no official reason is given, you learn that the cost of doing business in China is considerably less than the U.S., and you also learn that the Chinese government has manipulated its currency to make its goods unfairly cheap in U.S. markets while making U.S.-made goods unfairly expensive in Chinese markets.

Now imagine that you glance at the newspapers, tune in the occasional radio news at the top of the hour, check out a news site on the Web, watch some evening news on television two or three evenings a week, and in other ways try to keep up with all of the news and maybe even the political campaign.

How much would you hear the candidates discussing trade policy? Would you hear them mention Chinese currency policy and its impacts on U.S. trade deficits that are heading toward $1 trillion per year? Would you hear any data on how floods of artificially cheap imports were driving down prices in a concerted effort to undermine U.S. factories? Would you hear the candidates call for a review of trade policies, of U.S. tax laws and how they are anti-competitive to U.S.-made goods? Would you hear the candidates talk about the need for cost-benefit studies of U.S. regulatory frameworks and how they might affect the competitiveness of U.S. industries (and by the way, U.S. workers and jobs)?

Or would you hear more he-said-she-said about whose campaign took contributions from which interest groups?

A fundamental problem exists for the interests of working class voters. They often lack forceful champions to bring their issues front and center of today's noisy and contentious campaigns

Who then are the powerful social and political intermediaries to speak up on behalf of the working class voter? If the candidates do not focus their campaigns on these issues, who will work to coalesce a critical mass of public opinion on these issues and thereby compel the candidates to address them?

On the other side of the fence, many manufacturers and industrial groups have banded together to create political awareness and action regarding various issues, but even manufacturing groups are not always united on some issues. For example, multinational corporations may have different agendas on trade than their purely domestic counterparts, and may lobby for a much less forceful trade policy, and in fact they may be capitalizing on some of the same trends that are injuring the domestic workforce.

Within the National Association of Manufacturers a faction called the Domestic Manufacturers Group worked for nearly two years to get the national organization to endorse legislation that would take action against currency manipulation by U.S. trading partners. To date, the Domestic Manufacturers Group has had limited success, a fact which may lead to deeper divisions in a group whose very name implies a "national" mission.

During the Presidential election year of 2004 many of the issues related to jobs, paychecks and trade were raised by national and local candidates, particularly in districts which had been hard hit by plant closings and layoffs.

Some momentum was built along these lines, but for the most part these issues never rose to the top – they never became the compelling call to arms that could have produced a unified groundswell among a large cross-section of working class voters.

In the 2006 election we saw many competing factions, and we saw the craftsmanship of political consultants everywhere. Some campaigns were reduced to one-dimensional referenda on President Bush or the recycled boogey man of Democrats-as-tax-raisers.

Meanwhile, the pressures kept building along the major fault lines of American politics: peace and war, prosperity and hardship. A major thesis of these few chapters is that the fault line of prosperity and hardship is not being effectively addressed, either by the political campaigns or by the wheels of power in our government.

In Pennsylvania, the Keystone Research Center (KRC) reported that the gap between the state's low income families and high income families has been growing for two decades.[160] Whereas the incomes of the bottom fifth of Pennsylvania families grew by 22 percent from the early 1980s to the early 2000s, the incomes of the top fifth grew by 77 percent.[161] The average income of the bottom fifth was $18,548, compared to $129,371 for the top fifth.[162]

KRC notes that the wealthy end of this divide can be found in places such as Philadelphia's affluent suburbs, while economic stagnation takes hold in rural areas and the state's southwest.[163] KRC Economist Mark Price said, "Pennsylvania once had a strong middle class and one of the most equal state income distributions. It now has one of the more unequal."[164]

In Iowa, workers who had been displaced by jobs lost to effects of the North American Free Trade Agreement and who completed training under the Trade Adjustment Assistance Act found that their new jobs paid, on average, only 62 percent as much as the jobs they had lost.

A 38 percent pay cut is not just a pay cut. That cuts across every aspect of a family's financial security and is bound to exert profound influences on how these citizens view the political and personal landscape.

The pattern in Iowa is the same as elsewhere: good jobs that firmly establish the working class as part of the middle class are giving way to jobs that undermine the middle class status of these workers.

For example, the California economy added almost 600,000 jobs between November 2003 and May 2006, but more than one-third of them (35.6 percent) were in the lower paying retail trade and leisure and hospitality categories.[165] More than one-quarter of the job gains were in the construction industry, which is poised for major contraction as the housing-driven economy cools.[166] Meanwhile the number of jobs in manufacturing declined by more than 10 percent in the period, fueling the overall trend of flat or declining wages for the working class as a whole.[167]

Are there social and political pressures building as a result of lost jobs, lost benefits, flat or declining wages, and diminished prospects for American workers?

Yes.

So the questions arise, how can candidates or issues advocates move the concerns of the working class to center stage politically, and how can they get them translated into effective government policy?

Or play devil's advocate and ask, "What happens to the American economy and the American working class if we fail to address these issues?"

My personal prediction? Earthquake. Perhaps something equaling the scope of The Great Depression, which was at least a 7.5 on the Political Richter Scale.

Is that an overdramatic prediction? Maybe. But consider what could happen if these economic and social trends maintain or even gain momentum.

Consider what will happen if people continue to move from higher paying jobs to lower paying jobs, if they continue to move from jobs with medical insurance and pensions to jobs that offer nothing but substandard wages.

Consider what will happen if lifelong jobs with strong companies are replaced by a lifetime of moving from one dead-end, low-paying job to the next – to the point that workers never develop a sense of place or a sense of loyalty, and they in turn are treated as if their loyalty is beside the point.

Consider what will happen if some high profile American multinational companies create even the appearance that they place the interests of shareholders and profits ahead of the broader interests of their fellow Americans.

Consider what will happen if American workers perceive that neither America's corporate leadership nor its political leadership is committed to maintaining our industrial capacity and working class jobs.

Consider what will happen if America's elected representatives ignore – for a decade or a generation – the trends of lower wages and lower expectations, of greater income disparities and entire local or regional economies gutted and relegated to second class status in the American economy.

Consider what will happen if our economy is so hollowed out by the loss of industrial capacity that we lose the ability to make a full recovery from the next recession.

Consider what will happen if our national security is undermined by the loss of industrial capacity and the attendant research and development.

Amongst all the chatter and clatter and commotion of the election season, serious candidates are addressing such issues as our trade deficits, the loss of industrial capacity, the loss of American business to floods of unfair and illegal imports, and the outsourcing of jobs to Latin America and Asia. In a handful of districts around the country candidates have emerged who have placed fair trade enforcement at the top of their agenda, and this is a good start.

And if they are successful, either in getting elected or making these issues more prominent in the public debate, then we may begin to feel the first rumblings from working class voters.

The challenge is this: It takes enormous amounts of energy to create even small movements – much less creating major shifts in the political landscape.

Those who wish to create movement in the working class political landscape must strive to get people aware, involved, committed, and finally to push hard for movement and change.

I mentioned earlier the successes that Nucor, MSCI, and other groups have had in mobilizing thousands of citizens through nationwide series of town hall meetings. Contrary to the conventional wisdom of our time, I have found that citizens are interested in the issues – even the arcane issues such as currency manipulation and trade deficits. It may be too common these days to consign voters to a state of everlasting apathy, when instead we should be more willing to push and pull them into the issues and concerns of our day.

Just as important, many of the town hall meetings in which I have participated were heavily attended by elected officials. When you have United States Senators and Representatives drawn to the same meetings with state legislators, county and city council members, mayors and economic development leaders, you have created opportunities for the movement of ideas. But what's more important is that this generates a sense of shared ownership of the issues.

It is sometimes too easy for elected officials at the state and local level to dismiss international trade concerns, national energy policies or economic issues with the statement, "That's up to the federal government." But this overlooks the reality that state and local governments must bear many costs and burdens of job losses, falling incomes, loss of health insurance and other social and economic dislocations. By making every level of government a stakeholder in working class issues we can create a new dynamic in which all of our elected officials become inspired to get out in front of these issues and lead.

There really is something to be said for having local, state and federal officials gathered with large numbers of voters so that everyone can look at everyone else in the room and say to themselves, "I know what's going on with these issues. And I know that you know that I know."

This accomplishes a couple of things. One, it raises the stakes. If 1,500 or 2,000 people choose to come out on a cold, rainy night to learn about working class job losses (as they did in a 2006 Nucor town hall event in Upstate New York), then elected officials are provided with two choices: embrace the opportunity to lead or suffer potential consequences of inaction. By raising the stakes, such grass-roots actions help short-circuit the political temptation to throw a couple of sound bites at the issue and hope it goes away.

But something more begins to happen. In that funda-mental human way that still defies the glib assumptions of mass media, the word begins to get out. News still travels in ways not fully appreciated or acknowledged by the mass media. And this applies to both our unwired world and our wired world. When enough people get concerned and begin to speak out or take action at the grassroots, then the groundswell may be small at first, and the first sign just a faint rumble. But if it is ignored, it can grow to something much more powerful.

Americans still possess the capacity to be inspired and rallied to action. Even as our minds are numbed by the predictable he-said-she-said news coverage of political races we remain hungry for candidates and debates that challenge mind and muscle to move our nation forward.

Yes, the issues related to jobs, our economy and working class prospects are complex. Yes, they are tangled in such thorny areas as foreign policy, energy policy and fiscal policy. And yes, they require communication with voters that involves more than just a five-word campaign slogan.

The issues must be framed in ways that reflect local circumstances. What candidates *say* must reflect what voters *see* in their community and their workplace.

We must enlist and involve local leadership – grassroots leadership – even on global issues such as foreign trade. We must call on the working class voter to leave the sidelines and get in the game. (And while we're at it, let's challenge the leaders to show white collar Americans that they have a stake in the outcome as well.)

There is an opportunity to build a united force in American politics, and perhaps there is a desire among our citizens that can be tapped – a hunger to be united across lines of color, gender, creed and geography. And it is reasonable to ask, what is more unifying than our most common and basic human aspirations?

It is a fundamental American ambition – as individuals and as a nation – to build a solid middle class: not as something that is slipping from our grasp, but as something that we will keep within every American's reach.

As President Bush announced to the nation on the day after the 2006 midterm elections, Republicans took "a thumpin'" at the ballot box on election night.[168] However, he correctly pointed out that although the cumulative effect of the elections was a significant transfer of power to the Democratic party, the race-by-race results were very close. The fact of the matter is that the balance of power in this polarized American electorate is very tenuous. If the lessons of 2006 are not correctly understood, the potential for a another massive power shift will confront the new majority party.

First, it is important to have a measure of the 50:50 nature of the political balance of power prior to the 2006 election season. In round numbers, only 3 million votes separated George Bush and John Kerry, out of more than 121 million votes cast, so that President Bush won with 50.7 percent of the vote.

That looked like a landslide compared to the 2000 election between then Texas Governor George Bush and Vice President Al Gore, where only 543,895 votes separated winner from loser out of more than 100 million votes cast. George Bush won with 48.38 percent of the vote compared to Al Gore's 47.87 percent. (Ralph Nader polled 2.74 percent.)

The candidates for president work under the burden of being the combination bellwether, lightning rod, scapegoat, and standard bearer not only for their parties but for many of the issues that most concern voters. This race, these candidates, become emblematic of the fault lines that dissect American politics and American voters: war versus peace, prosperity versus hardship.

Consider, for instance that going into the 2004 elections the Republicans controlled a bare majority of state legislatures across the country, with Democrats controlling the fewest state legislatures in half a century. In that election year about 80 percent of the 7,382 state legislative seats were contested in 44 states, and Republicans held 50.3 percent of the 7,333 partisan seats while Democrats controlled 49.4 percent. Third party legislators held 0.2 percent. It is hard to shave a majority much closer than that. And overall the two main parties were dealing with divided governance among the various political branches in 29 states, where neither party had exclusive control of the governor's office and both legislative chambers.

Although these governments often take a back seat to the Presidential and Congressional races, this recent trend among and within the states shows clearly that a change of heart among a relatively concentrated bloc of voters could create major shifts in the balance of power, within the various states and nationwide.

In the 2006 mid-term elections, 83 percent of the state legislative seats were contested across a nation where 20 legislatures were controlled by Republicans, 19 were controlled by Democrats, and 10 were split. (The unicameral Nebraska legislature is non-partisan.)

The National Council of State Legislatures reported that 10 states had the potential for major movement along the Republican-Democrat fault lines of state politics:

- The Iowa House of Representatives had a two-seat Republican majority, and the Senate was tied;
- In Montana the House was tied, and both parties were fielding candidates in 82 of the 100 races;
- North Carolina's House leadership was undergoing ethics investigations while Republicans needed to gain only four seats to claim a majority;
- In Colorado, Democrats had a one-seat majority in the Senate and four-seat majority in the House;
- Control of the Indiana House had switched in six of the past nine elections and was considered up for grabs in 2006 as Republicans clung to a four-seat majority;
- In Minnesota, Democrats had to gain just two seats to control the House;
- Maine voters have a tradition of ticket splitting, which made it difficult to predict whether Democrats would keep their one-seat majority in the Senate or three-seat majority in the House;
- All seven retiring Oklahoma Senators were Democrats, and Republicans needed to pick up only three seats to control that chamber;
- Oregon Democrats believed they had a good opportunity to pick up four seats and control that state's House of Representatives; and
- In Tennessee Republicans had controlled the Senate for the past two years – after more than a century out

of power, and rigorously defended a slim, three-seat majority.[169]

All of these fragile majorities added up to a close, hard-fought contest between the two main parties, because the prize for victory was considerable power, both at the state and national levels. The swing of a few Congressional seats and relatively small numbers of state legislative seats would result in significant shifts of power to either party. This is exactly what happened in the 2006 midterm elections.

On the federal level, Democrats took control of the U.S. Senate by a 51-49 margin, picking up six seats. Democrats gained over 30 seats in the U.S. House to form a slim majority. Democratic governors were elected in six new states, giving them a 28 to 22 advantage in the executive offices of the states. Republicans did not manage to gain a single governor's office. Democrats gained control of almost 335 new state legislative seats, taking control of both houses of the legislature in 24 states (up from 19), reducing Republican control to 16 states (down from 20), and splitting control of 9 states.[170]

The question is: what swept the Democrats into power?

Let's start with what did not happen.

First, Democrats did not suddenly become the dominant party in American politics. In other words, there is no strong indicator that Republican voters were flocking to the Democratic party. While Democrats made tremendous gains in real power by seizing a large number of state and federal offices, the margin of victory in many races was exceptionally close, and the opinion polling leading up to the elections reflects this. It would not take a substantial shift in opinion to reverse the gains of the Democratic party in 2008.

In the month prior to the 2004 elections, a slim majority of American voters – 46 percent – expressed a preference for Democratic-controlled Congress, compared to 44 percent who preferred a Republican Congress.[171] Immediately following the 2004 elections, which included the close and hotly contested Presidential race and resulted in the continued Republican control of Congress, the number of Americans preferring to see the Democrats control Congress increased to 51 percent; 44 percent still preferred a Republican Congress.[172]

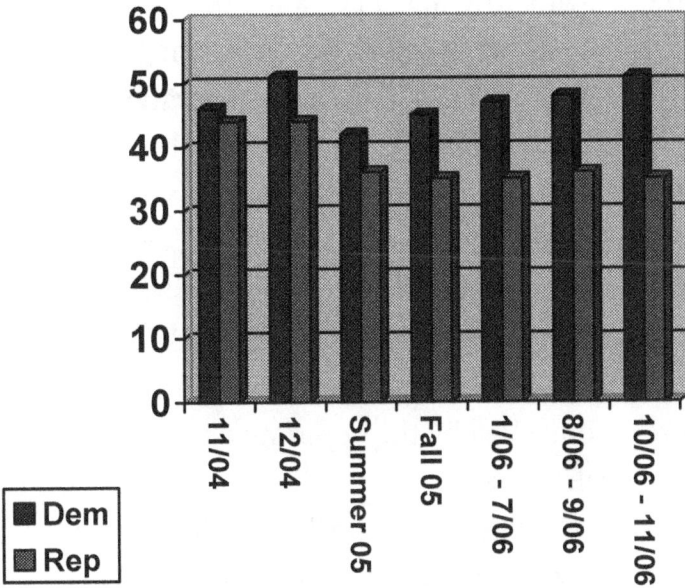

Fig. 5-1: Which Party Would You Prefer Control Congress?[173]

By the fall of 2005, as the previous year's elections faded from the public's memory, voters preferred Democratic control 45 to 35 percent.[174] Almost 15 percent more Americans had become undecided about their preference for party control. But unlike Democrats, Republicans never regained the 9 percent of these undecided voters that had previously favored a Republican-controlled Congress.[175] By the month leading up to the 2006 midterm elections, only 35 percent of voters preferred to see Republicans in control of Congress.[176] Whereas preference for a Democratic Congress had returned to 51 percent.[177]

The key here is to realize that if there had been a national shift in voters' sympathy and allegiance to the Democratic Party, one would expect to see an accompanying increase in expressed voter preference for a Democratic-controlled Congress. And yet the polling data indicates that Democrats never managed to garner more support than what they had immediately after their defeat in 2004. Rather, it was the incumbent Republican majority that managed to quickly lose a quarter of its supporters, and never recovered. But these dissatisfied voters did not begin expressing a preference to see a Congress controlled by the opposing party. They merely expressed no preference at all.

Second, we see a similar result when we look at polls that ask for which party voters intended to cast their ballot.

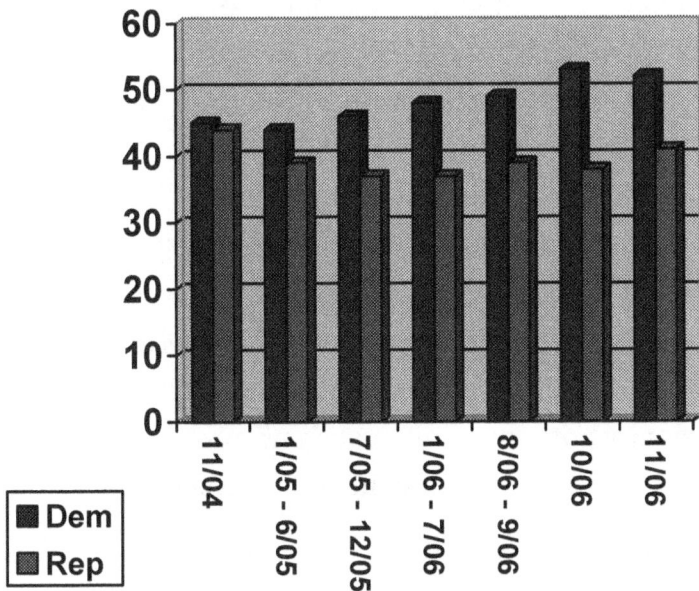

Fig. 5-2: For Which Party Do You Intend to Vote?[178]

In the month prior to the 2004 election, 44 percent of voters indicated they would vote for a Republican for Congress, and 45 percent said they would vote for Democrat.[179] During 2005, the average polling results indicated that 38 percent of voters intended to vote for the Republican candidates for Congress, and 46 percent intended to vote for the Democrats.[180] By the week before the 2006 midterm elections, 41 percent of voters had indicated they would vote Republican, and 52 percent indicated they would vote Democratic.[181]

Once again, there was no noticeable defection of those voters who indicated that they would vote for the Republican candidate prior to the 2004 election. Rather, the numbers depict Democrats gaining votes from the voters who had not decided one way or another since the 2004 elections. These voters will have no compunction about changing their vote if their needs are not addressed by this new majority.

Third, anti-incumbent sentiment was not the deciding factor in the Congressional races. Leading up to the 2006 midterm elections, 53 percent of Americans indicated that their mood was "anti-incumbent."[182] Only 29 percent were "pro-incumbent."[183] And yet when asked whether their Congressional incumbents deserved to be re-elected, in the month before the election, 40 percent of voters responded "yes" – a significant jump from just a few months prior to the election day, and almost the same as voter sentiment in the summer of 2005. [184]

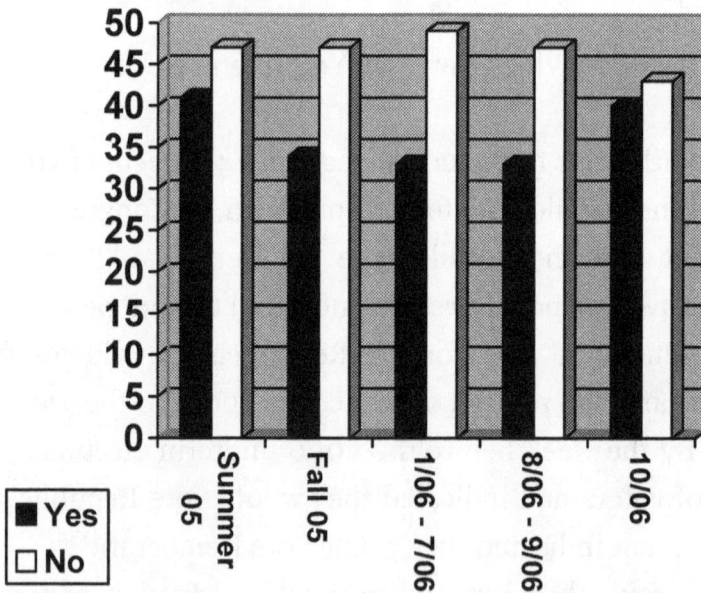

Fig. 5-3: Does Your Incumbent Deserve to Be Re-elected?[185]

In fact, when voters were asked specifically whether they would like to see their representative re-elected (as opposed to whether the representative deserved reelection), voters consistently responded almost 2:1 that they would prefer that their Congressional representatives be re-elected.[186] One would expect to see more extreme anti-incumbent sentiment if a "throw the bums out" mentality had been the impetus behind the midterm ballots.

The point is, these polls don't tell the story they were imagined to: the fact that a majority of American voters were indicating a preference for a hypothetical Democratic candidate over a hypothetical Republican candidate and were fed up with the incumbent majority did not directly translate into more votes for Democrats than in 2004. As in past races, the closer election day approached, the more poll margins shrank, and uncertainty grew when voters were asked to consider their specific incumbent.

Such is the nature of answers to general questions versus specific ones. Candidates that base their campaign strategy on trying to avoid being seen as part of the "bad" majority, end up using those contrived special interest sound bites I mentioned earlier. Avoiding appearances with the President will not save a candidate who fails to address the core issues that affect the lives of the voters.

I posit that candidates – from either party – who address the issues of America's working class will gain a competitive advantage in today's split electorate – just as Reagan and Roosevelt did in previous eras. And the core issues to America's working class are their jobs and the ability of those jobs to give them the means to provide for their families.

This is evident in what we saw in the 2006 midterm elections.

How did working class Americans generally size up the situation leading into the midterm elections of 2006? What did it look like "out there" in the field? It is fair to say that for incumbents, job security in many districts was a false security. Times appeared to be tough for incumbents. There was a war on. Terrorists were on the loose. Corruption was rampant. Incomes were stagnant. Prices were rising. Good jobs were being replaced by second rate jobs. Many people had more or less abandoned the search for a job. Mill towns, factory towns, foundry towns, lumber towns and high-tech towns often had one thing in common: the jobs were gone and they would not be coming back.

Families were uprooting, cutting back, selling out, and in some cases giving up.

There is no question that the recession of 2001 hit working class Americans hard. Not only did they lose their jobs, many lost their careers. Manufacturing workers at steel mills, auto factories and textile mills have walked away from workplaces that were family traditions for two or three generations. The "jobless recovery" following the recession has been well documented, and for many its effects continue to be felt by breadwinners and their families alike.

Nor did working Americans perceive things to be getting any better. This perception had significant repercussions in many Congressional races, which were the national focus for the 2006 midterm election cycle. However, voters did not simply lay blame at the feet of a party or the incumbents and vote accordingly. Instead, voters looked to see how candidates responded to the issues that the voters perceived to be key to "making things better." This is a trend that can be seen developing in the 2004 election cycle.

In 2004, the John J. Heldrich Center for Workforce Development at Rutgers University reported study findings that in the first three years of this century nearly one in five American workers had been laid off, with the big majority of them receiving no advance notice, no severance pay and no career counseling from their employers.[187] And even for those workers who escaped layoff, one-third of them worked for companies where co-workers had been laid off. [188]

As part of the same study, the Heldrich Center reported that only 7 percent of workers said that President Bush was doing an excellent job of handling jobs-related issues, while 32 percent of workers said he was doing a poor job. [189]

At the time of this study, long-term unemployment, the jobless recovery, and all of the attendant stresses and strains were a significant burden on the American workforce. And even before the national divide began to emerge over the war in Iraq, the issues related to jobs and the economy began to compete with terrorism to be among the pre-eminent political issues of our times.

In the months before the 2004 elections the International Association of Machinists and Aerospace Workers (IAM) reported that more than 25 percent of American families surveyed had experienced a job loss in the previous two years.[190] The study also focused on Illinois, Ohio, Wisconsin, and Washington, to determine voter attitudes toward the job situation and the candidates.[191]

In Ohio, where Rust Belt blue collar workers were heavily courted by both parties in 2004, the survey revealed that 36 percent of the families who had experienced a job loss in the previous two years still had a family member unemployed as the election approached.[192] In Illinois, the figure was even more dramatic, at 41 percent.[193] The IAM reported, "Despite the traditional alliance between blue-collar workers and Democratic candidates, the survey found a huge reservoir of potential votes for whichever candidate will act decisively on their behalf."[194]

The union's president, Tom Buffenbarger, said, "The blue collar vote in these four core states is still up for grabs. The candidate who ultimately connects with these workers could ride that support all the way to the White House. The candidate who ignores them will do so at his own expense."[195]

In the closing days of the campaign, Ohio received the full-court press from both candidates, and out of more than 5.6 million votes cast, the President's winning margin was just 118,599 – a two percent margin. If just 11 votes in each of Ohio's 11,360 precincts had gone the other way, the state's 20 electoral votes would have gone to Democrat challenger John Kerry.

Another sign of just how close things got in Ohio was the heated effort mounted post-election by some Kerry supporters to discredit the Ohio vote count, along much the same lines of the close and decisive Florida vote in 2000.

Ohio made an interesting study in the months leading up to the 2004 election also. In July the CNN/USA Today/-Gallup poll showed Kerry with a lead among likely voters of

48 percent to 43 percent over the President, a lead which had been reversed by the first week of September to a 52 percent to 43 percent advantage for President Bush. Then by mid-October the same poll showed Kerry with a one-point advantage.

In mid-October, just a couple of weeks before the election, a majority of Ohio voters surveyed for the Chicago Tribune and WGN-TV said they did not approve of the President's handling of the situation in Iraq (53 percent) and the economy (52 percent). Just over half (52 percent) expressed approval for his handling of the war on terrorism. Likewise, an ABC News Poll taken at that same time reported that 54 percent of registered voters surveyed said that "most people in Ohio" were not as well off financially as they were in 2001 when Bush became President. Only 10 percent indicated they were better off financially.

Given polling data such as this, it is easy enough to see why challenger Kerry and his campaign worked so diligently in Ohio, right up to the eve of the election.

An interesting footnote to the survey scene of 2004 is the survey conducted in March of that year by The Harris Poll. A more than two-thirds majority disagreed with the statement that "it is good for the U.S. economy when American companies use less expensive workers in countries like China and India to do work previously done at a higher cost in this country."

A majority almost as large, 64 percent, thought it was a bad idea to use Chinese workers to manufacture things previously made in the U.S., and a somewhat smaller number, 59 percent, said the same about moving manufacturing jobs to Mexico. When one enters an area that is dependent on these type of jobs, and one initiates an educational campaign to demonstrate that the reason for the jobs moving to places like China is due in part to illegal trade tactics and our own country's refusal to seek enforcement, the result is the growth of tremendous grassroots opposition to ambivalent incumbents.

When asked which Presidential candidate would have the better policies to address this issue, President Bush got the endorsement of only 24 percent of those surveyed – less even than the 26 percent who responded "not sure." John Kerry got the vote of confidence of 32 percent of those surveyed, and 18 percent said neither candidate would be likely to have the better policies.

Clearly, there was a large opportunity for a candidate on these issues, more than six months ahead of the election, but it is not clear from either the vote or other surveys that either candidate reached the full potential of the opportunity.

Exit polling data from 2004 provides an interesting perspective on this pivotal electoral state and perhaps provide clues for upcoming races and opportunities for candidates who are trying to bring the blue collar vote into focus.

As reported by CNN.com, exit polls of 2,020 Ohio voters in 2004 revealed the following:

- Voters with household income below $50,000 supported Kerry, 58 percent to 42 percent, while just the opposite held true for voters with household income above $50,000, who supported Bush by an equal margin.

- Of the 24 percent of voters who identified the economy and jobs as the most important issue, an overwhelming majority of 83 percent voted for Kerry, compared to 17 percent who voted for Bush. It is significant to note that the economy and jobs topped the list of reasons cited by voters – more than moral values (23 percent), terrorism (17 percent), Iraq (13 percent) and other issues such as health care, education and taxes. (This statistic clearly foreshadowed the growing concern and importance of job and economy to the electorate.)

- With no cross tabulation it's impossible to determine overlap, but it's worth noting that when asked to name the most important quality by the candidate of their choice, the most chosen quality was "will bring change," which was cited by 24 percent of voters, who went 93 percent for Kerry and only 6 percent for Bush.

- Among voters whose financial situation was better in 2004 than 2000, 87 percent voted for Bush, but among voters whose financial situation was worse in 2004 than 2000, it was almost the opposite, with 85 percent voting for Kerry and 15 percent voting for Bush. Among voters whose financial situation was the same, Bush edged Kerry 55 percent to 45 percent.

- Perhaps not surprising in light of the above, voters who said the job situation in their area had grown worse supported Kerry 75 percent and Bush 25 percent. Those who cited a better job situation in 2004 supported the President 93 percent, to 7 percent for Kerry. Those who said the job situation was about the same supported Bush, 77 percent to Kerry's 23 percent.

- Looking at the state economy overall, voters who characterized the economy as "poor" voted 90 percent for Kerry and 10 percent for Bush. Voters who said "not so good" voted 63 percent for Kerry, 36 percent for Bush. Those who rated the economy "good" supported the incumbent 86 percent, to Kerry's 13 percent. A statistically insignificant number of voters rated the Ohio economy as "excellent."
- John Kerry carried the 17 percent of voters who were union members with 60 percent of their vote, compared to Bush's 39 percent. Among union households Kerry did almost as well, with 58 percent of the vote, compared to Bush's 42 percent. Voters from non-union households supported the President, 53 percent to Kerry's 46 percent.
- Kerry garnered a substantial majority among Independents, with 59 percent of their vote compared to Bush's 40 percent.

An Opinion Research Poll conducted in September for CNN reported that 28 percent of Americans said that the economy would be most important in determining their 2006 vote for Congress – three percent more than Iraq and ten percent more than terrorism. In the same poll a majority of voters, 56 percent, rated the economy as "poor."

A Fox News/Opinion Dynamics poll taken the last week of August 2006 showed that 23 percent of voters ranked the economy at the top of their concerns – 9 percent more than terrorism and 11 percent more than the war in Iraq.

A survey by Greenberg Quinlan Rosner (commissioned by the Democratic candidate) asked those surveyed to respond to two statements by indicating which statement most closely reflected their own views, even if neither statement was "exactly right."

Statement one: "The Democrat says, incomes have been stagnant for five years and people are under great financial pressure, but Bush and the Republicans have only cut taxes for the wealthiest. For them, the economy is great. They've sided with the drug and oil companies who've pumped up health care and gas prices and given tax breaks for companies that outsource jobs. I'll work to get health care and gas prices down, cut middle class taxes and reward companies that create jobs here."

Statement two: "The Republican says, our economy is strong and our tax cuts for families and businesses made this possible. Last year our economy grew faster than any industrialized nation's in the world. We created over 5 million new jobs over the last two and half years and homeownership is at the highest level ever. The economy is moving in the right direction and none of us can afford the Democrats' new tax increases."

Now we recognize that this is not so much an exercise in objective, precise, scientific measurement of how voters might vote as it is an exercise in testing the political "message." But here's how 1,000 likely voters responded to those two messages in June 2006:

- 47 percent said the Democrat statement "strongly" came closer to their own view, and 10 percent said the statement "not so strongly" came closer to their own view.
- 32 percent said the Republican statement strongly came closer to their own view, and 8 percent said the statement not so strongly came closer to their own view.

Without arguing the merits of the survey methods or the wording of the statements, it is nevertheless instructive to consider these percentages and reconsider some of the perspectives raised earlier about the jobs and personal financial situations faced by America's working class.

One thing is clear, America's working class, along with all other groups of voters, certainly were afforded ample opportunity to participate in polls and surveys about the 2006 Congressional elections.

After the 2006 elections, national exit polling showed that the economy was the number one issue that concerned voters. Media outlets widely reported that the exit polling showed that corruption was predominant on voters' minds. However, this analysis of the polling data accounts only for the voter response, "extremely important." Corruption (41%) was considered "extremely important" to the vote of 2% more people than the economy (39%).[196]

In your vote for U.S. House, how important was the economy?

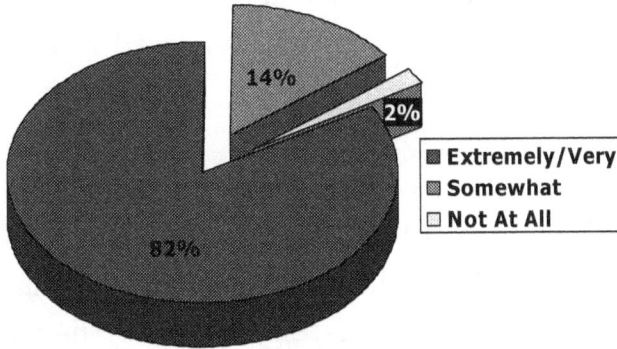

Fig. 5-4 National Exit Polling, 2006 Elections

However, when totaling the responses of both "extremely" and "very important" (corruption 33%; economy 43%), only 74% of respondents found corruption very and extremely important, 8% less than those who felt the same about their vote and the economy.[197] Clearly, the state of the economy played a crucial role in the decisions made by voters on election day.

I'd like to elaborate on this point by examining a number of the Congressional districts that served as the field lab for our research in the 2006 midterm elections. We saw similar patterns emerge in states and economies as diverse as Iowa and North Carolina.

First, we looked at six districts where incumbents were defeated in 2006: Indiana's 2nd, 8th, and 9th districts, Iowa's 2nd, Kentucky's 3rd, and North Carolina's 11th districts.

All of these Congressional districts have a workforce that is composed of a percentage of manufacturing jobs equal to or higher than the average for the United States – 11.9 percent. In fact, approximately 19 percent of the total workforce of these districts is employed in manufacturing. All of these states have lost significant numbers of manufacturing jobs: Indiana has lost 14% of its manufacturing jobs, or 90,900 jobs, since 1998; Iowa has lost 7%, or 19,000 jobs; Kentucky has lost 16%, or 48,500 jobs; and North Carolina has lost 31% of its manufacturing job, a total of 246,200 jobs since 1998.[198] The median family income for these districts is almost $5,000 less than the national average, $55,832.[199] And the median per capita income is almost $3,000 less in these districts than the national average of $25,035. [200] The voters in these districts have felt the direct effects of the dismantling of our manufacturing economy because of the illegal trade practices of foreign competitors and their sponsor nations.

How have these losses evidenced themselves in the electorate? First of all, across these districts, local city and county officials spoke up for their communities, urging their state and federal representatives – and candidates for federal office – to take a leadership position on defending fair trade principles. Take for example, Cherokee County, North Carolina. The westernmost county in North Carolina, Cherokee County is home to just over 24,000 people. Manufacturing accounts for about 17% of the jobs in the county, and is critical to the stability of the economy. County leaders decided to make their voices heard, and on October 3, 2006, they passed the following resolution:

A RESOLUTION

TO REQUEST THAT THE NORTH CAROLINA GENERAL ASSEMBLY, AND THE NORTH CAROLINA CONGRESSIONAL DELEGATION CONTINUE TO SUPPORT THE FAMILIES OF NORTH CAROLINA, TO SUPPORT STRONG TRADE POLICY, AND TO TAKE SWIFT AND RESPONSIVE ACTIONS TO HALT UNLAWFUL BARRIERS TO FAIR AND FREE TRADE.

Whereas, $136 billion in wages are expected to shift from the U.S. to low cost nations by 2015; these American jobs go to workers who are paid just pennies per hour in unsafe conditions, and who receive no medical or other benefits; and

Whereas, Manufacturing is a vital part of the American economy, providing tens of millions of families with jobs; and

Whereas, America manufacturing creates, on average, four indirect and support jobs for every one job it creates; and

Whereas, the United States trade deficit has been fluctuating between $60 billion and $70 billion per month, and surpassed $725 billion in 2005; and

Whereas, Industries that once were the pride of their communities and employed generations of the same families have lost jobs to foreign nations where labor is artificially cheap, where currency is illegally manipulated, and where environmental standards are not enforced, rendering domestic manufacturing unable to compete; and

Whereas, North Carolina's manufacturing sector, as well as suppliers and ancillary businesses, has lost over 253,000 jobs in the past decade; and

Whereas, North Carolina is the state most affected by outsourcing; one in five North Carolina manufacturing jobs has been lost to overseas competition; and

Whereas, Manufacturing employs about 1,500 people in the Cherokee County, accounting for 17 percent of the jobs in the county.

Now, Therefore, Be it resolved by the Cherokee County Commissioners:

That the County Commissioners of Cherokee County, on behalf of North Carolina's citizens and business, by this resolution, encour-
age the United States Department of the Trea-
sury to stake a strong position on behalf of fair
trade. Free trade can only succeed if the rule of
law is diligently applied; and

Be it Further Resolved

That the County Commissioners of Cherokee County urge citizens of North Carolina to
support strong trade policy and act in a manner
that can best help preserve, protect and defend
the vital manufacturing jobs of North Carolina.

What could the county commissioners in Cherokee
County hope to achieve with such a resolution? It has no
binding legal authority – the state and federal represent-
tatives of this county are not suddenly under obligation to
follow the dictates of the county commission. The power of
such a resolution comes from its expression of the will of that
community. And when the chorus is joined by other voices –
like the people of Graham, Clay, and Polk counties – the call
to the officials who represent these communities becomes
impossible to ignore.

Second, these districts saw an average increase in voter
turnout of almost 8.5% - over 16,000 votes per district. The
margin of victory in the majority of the house races in the
2006 midterm elections was well below 16,000 votes – the

influx of energized voters could very well have made the difference in these elections.

Third, the number of DMQ voters with a direct stake in the manufacturing economy in each of these districts exceeded the margin of victory.

- North Carolina 11: DMQ = 65,757; Margin of victory = 18,000 votes
- Indiana 8: DMQ = 97,568; Margin of victory = 46,464
- Iowa 2: DMQ = 87,569; Margin of victory = 5,711
- Indiana 2: DMQ = 131,961; Margin of victory = 15,145
- Indiana 9: DMQ = 126,207; Margin of victory = 9,682
- Kentucky 3: DMQ = 58,140; Margin of victory = 5,890

Manufacturing employees and their families are a decisive force in all of these districts.

However, this analysis is not limited to the upset of incumbents, nor to the election of Democrats. In Illinois's 6th Congressional District, similar issue patterns emerged in the race for the seat being vacated by retiring Representative Henry Hyde. Like its neighbor, Indiana, Illinois has been a traditional manufacturing juggernaut and a state where American workers had established themselves solidly in America's middle class.

According to a report by the Center for Tax and Budget Accountability and Northern Illinois University, the blue collar voters of Illinois are facing many of the same challenges as their fellow citizens across the U.S., including:

- An economy that is growing more slowly than the U.S. as a whole;
- The loss of almost a quarter of a million manufacturing jobs over a decade and a half;

- Most of the jobs replacing the manufacturing jobs have come in professional and business services, which as a category pays 4.6 percent less than manufacturing, and in education, health services and leisure and hospitality, which pay on average more than 29 percent less than manufacturing;
- A 7.6 percent decline in median wages for men from 1980 to 2004, and a decline in the state's median household income;
- A 15 percent decline in the portion of the workforce covered by private medical insurance, fewer workers covered by private pension plans; and
- Projections that less than half of future jobs will pay wages that exceed the current average wages, resulting in a state economy that will create more low-wage jobs than high-wage jobs.[201]

The Illinois's 6th is a suburban district in a city and a region where manufacturing has been a cornerstone of the economy. Manufacturing jobs account for over 15% of the employment in this district. The district provides an interesting study of the extent to which personal, family, and national economics will influence a campaign, where manufacturing is an important component of the local economy and the overall district demographics are solidly middle class.

In light of manufacturing's contributions to the district's economy, it is noteworthy that much of the media coverage of the race through the early and middle going did not focus more on issues relating to the struggles of this sector. Much of the coverage centered on the war in Iraq. Immigration also figured into the election, and I have already alluded to this as a back-door pocketbook issue because of the belief that floods of illegal immigrants in certain districts can depress wages.

However, local domestic manufacturers began to engage the candidates on the issues that mattered most to them – trade policy, energy costs, and excessive regulation.

The Democratic candidate, Major Tammy Duckworth, was an Army helicopter pilot who was injured in the Iraq war when her helicopter was ambushed. The resulting explosion cost her both her legs. She received a Purple Heart for her sacrifice and service. Clearly, Major Duckworth was a candidate that inspired respect, and made a natural spokesperson for an issue that everyone anticipated would be the centerpiece of the 2006 elections – the Iraq war. In fact, Major Duckworth focused most of her campaign energy around issues related to that subject – the handling of the war, health care for veterans, and military spending.

As I mentioned earlier, Peter Roskam, the Republican candidate, chose to highlight the plight of manufacturing workers in Illinois, stating: "We have a serious problem in Illinois. We lost over 180,000 manufacturing jobs - we can't just let that happen."[202] Roskam won this district by just 5,000 votes.

There are 51,767 manufacturing workers in Illinois's 6th district. Using our DMQ formula, we determine that 88,003 eligible voters have a direct stake in manufacturing. We have a quantifiable DMQ voting block that is thirteen times greater than Roskam's margin of victory in 2006. Voter turnout in Illinois's 6th district was up almost 1,700 votes since 2002 – just over one-third of the votes Roskam needed to win the district. A candidate willing to embrace the working class in this district could ensure his or her continued employment by the people of Illinois.

As in our other districts of focus, significant numbers of voters had – and still have – a direct stake in issues that are of consequence to working class citizens. The reason why these voters mobilized to support a Republican on a day of Democratic victory is clear. The voters were engaged on the issues that mattered most to them.

PART 6

RUMBLINGS

"Each time a man stands up for an ideal, or acts to improve the lot of others, or strikes out against injustice, he sends forth a tiny ripple of hope, and crossing each other from a million different centers of energy and daring those ripples build a current which can sweep down the mightiest walls of oppression and resistance."

— *Robert F. Kennedy, 1966*

The political landscape is beginning to shift and rumble somewhat in response to the issues and social changes that we have discussed. We saw and heard these shifts and rumbles in certain states and districts in the 2004 election, and we are seeing others take shape in the 2006 mid-term elections.

I'd like to draw on a pair of examples at the national level to serve as "bookends" to the discussion: the two free trade agreements known as NAFTA and CAFTA.

The 1992 Presidential election and the North American Free Trade Agreement (NAFTA) provided some indelible images in the minds of Americans who were following the campaigns.

The competent, patrician incumbent, President George H.W. Bush appeared to be somewhat blindsided by the nation's economy as a political issue. Independent challenger

Ross Perot created memorable images in voters' minds with his flip charts and his prediction that in the wake of the North American Free Trade Agreement Americans would hear the "giant sucking sound" of U.S. jobs going to Mexico.

Meanwhile, Democrat challenger Bill Clinton worked to focus voters' attentions on the problems with the U.S. economy ("It's the economy, stupid") without necessarily showing his hand on NAFTA.

Clinton gained support from union leaders without immediately making known his position on NAFTA.[203] This created an opportunity for the unions to influence Clinton's stand on the agreement, which he ultimately decided to support.[204]

Clinton received 55 percent of the union vote, with Bush and Perot more or less splitting the rest of the union vote with 24 percent and 21 percent respectively.[205]

It is reasonable enough to chalk up Clinton's union support to the long-standing tradition of support for the Democrat Party and its pro-union stands on various issues.[206] Clinton was able to maintain a certain level of support through his endorsement of training programs and other government remedies for any ill effects from the free trade agreement. [207]

It is useful to consider as well that Clinton had the luxury of letting his opponent position NAFTA as a tool of job creation and economic growth, which could then be co-opted once the election was over and used to solidify some Democrat support for the treaty.

It may be fair to say that the single most effective "sound bite" from that debate and the one that has become most emblematic of free trade agreements was Perot's "giant sucking sound" prediction. Even today, almost a decade and a half later it is still the single most recognizable catch phrase regarding globalization and American jobs.

So it is not without a touch of irony to note that by 2003, the company founded and built by Perot, Electronic Data Systems (EDS), was profiled by Forbes Magazine under the headline, "Giant Sucking Sound," in which the magazine reported that EDS had begun shipping a variety of white collar jobs to India.[208]

Just this year, Business Week noted that EDS "all but invented the information outsourcing industry" as the magazine reported the company in recent years has struggled against competitors because it failed to move more work out of the U.S. sooner.[209] The article reports that the company is undertaking major expansion and acquisitions in Asia, with its Indian workforce expected to grow from 3,000 to 20,000 by the end of 2006.[210]

Today "that giant sucking sound" remains a sound bite landmark of American politics, long after Ross Perot has taken his hat from the ring. The sucking sound itself seems to have grown so loud and sustained that it has enveloped even the company that Perot founded and the industry on which he help build. Although Perot is no longer relevant to the major political contests of our times, his cultural artifact remains relevant indeed.

Judging by what happened with CAFTA in 2005, Perot's assessment can be viewed as either a political prophecy, or, at the very least, an albatross around the necks of free trade agreements, because his idea stuck.

At any rate, the Central American Free Trade Agreement was born into a very different world than its ancestor, the North American Free Trade Agreement. Although there was not universal agreement on whether that giant sucking sound was in fact due to NAFTA or similar agreements, there was a growing awareness that jobs were leaving the country in quantity and quality, and the departure of these jobs was leaving too many workers in the lurch.

As a result, the pressure and the competition for "yes" and "no" votes became intense during the summer of 2005. No President, Senator or Representative would be permitted to duck the question.

The Bush administration lobbied members of the U.S. House intensely after the Senate had approved CAFTA, and opponents were lobbying just as hard. For a while during that summer, CAFTA held its own with Iraq as a topic for disagreement and discussions. And when it came down to a vote in the House of Representatives, CAFTA's fate hung in the balance, literally until the midnight hour.

The House voted 217 to 215 to approve CAFTA, such a narrow margin that the change of one vote would have resulted in a tie, and the failure of the measure. The distinction of casting the deciding vote went to Representative Robin Hayes, a North Carolina Republican who had staunchly opposed the agreement up to the day before the vote.

As reported in the press, the story took many shapes. One, it was a story of political arm-twisting, deal-making and persuasion. Two, it was a story of Presidential prestige on the line. And, three, it was a story of how things such as CAFTA can take on chameleon-like qualities in the swirl and storm of political debate.

CAFTA meant many things to many people. It was essential to national security and manageable immigration for the hemisphere. It was an enemy of environmental protection and labor rights. It was a relatively minor trade agreement and not deserving of the controversy. Or it was yet another opportunity to draw a line in the sand against further job losses.

I raise the NAFTA-CAFTA story to illustrate this point: the earth has moved. Along the fault line of prosperity and hard times parts of the landscape have been heaved up and parts have been knocked down. CAFTA was not "The Big One" of course, but the fact that a sitting President with his party in the majority in both houses of Congress had to pull out all of the stops to pass a relatively small-caliber trade agreement makes it clear to this observer that there are growing rumblings among working class Americans and their elected representatives.

Everyone involved in American politics should begin to assign new importance and focus urgent attention on this issue – and any issue – that has a direct bearing on the American working class. And by "everyone," I mean the parties and their leadership, candidates and would-be candidates, pundits, courtiers, consultants, pollsters and the entire political establishment, both in and out of power.

We should be aware that the ground is shifting beneath our feet. Also, we should be neither afraid nor comforted by the fact that this has happened many times before in our nation's history. The first question to ask ourselves as we feel the ground move: Are we standing still or moving forward?

A century ago Theodore Roosevelt was the undisputed master of the "Bully Pulpit" and he strode across the stage as the unquestioned central figure in American politics. Moreover, for the first time in history, an American President occupied the place of prominence on the global political stage.

His times bear more than a little resemblance to our own. The U.S. was newly asserting itself as a military power and diplomatic heavyweight, and had recently fought a war that some thought based on dubious grounds, but one which was designed to put a rival in check.

In that era, Roosevelt's militarism may have been a somewhat easier sell, but it firmly established his stature as a fighter, which he shrewdly used to advance what he called the "Square Deal."

Just as today, the world economy was undergoing a period of rapid growth and change at the turn of the 20th century. Roosevelt, the "Rough Rider," added to his fame with the charge on San Juan Hill. Roosevelt, the "trust-buster," earned loyalty from the working class troops at home when he took on some of the country's most powerful corporations, launching anti-trust suits and even persuading Congress to create federal agencies to regulate the growing power of corporate interests.

In a letter to Sir Edward Gray in 1913, after he had left office, Roosevelt wrote, "We demand that big business give the people a square deal; in return we must insist that when anyone engaged in big business honestly endeavors to do right he shall himself be given a square deal."[211]

Ten years earlier, in a speech given at the New York State Fair Roosevelt said, "We must treat each man on his worth and merits as a man. We must see that each is given a square deal, because he is entitled to no more and should receive no less."[212]

These remarks really get to the heart of Roosevelt's view of the nation and its people. The Square Deal was never intended to be a spoils system or a redistribution scheme, but was grounded in Roosevelt's staunch and clear view that good citizens should expect to be given a good chance by the system, and that they in turn were obligated to the system to be good citizens. He was an individualist, who saw himself as the leader of a nation of individualists.

Since Roosevelt's day, many Americans have worked to polarize voters and interests along a divide between business and labor. Theodore Roosevelt tried to balance the interests of both, recognizing that the labor movement could not give itself over to the "mob rule" that he distrusted, and that business could not hope to profit or thrive in a system where workers were not given a Square Deal.

He became a champion of abolishing child labor, and of instituting unemployment insurance and pensions, which are perfectly mainstream positions today, but which were not embraced by some business interests in his own time.

Roosevelt's efforts were significant for at least two reasons. First, he demonstrated to both business and labor that each could not ultimately expect to prosper at the long-term expense of the other. But just as important, he began to synthesize a variety of policies that people in the working class could identify as in their overarching interests.

Some of these are obvious, such as strengthening the ability of labor to negotiate and organize on behalf of workers. Others are somewhat removed from working class bread-and-butter issues, but are significant. Under Roosevelt's powerful leadership, average Americans saw their government step in and regulate the safety and hygiene of food and drug production. They saw their government set aside national parklands for the enjoyment of all citizens.

It is not a stretch to say that in the particulars, and in very broad strokes, working Americans saw in Theodore Roosevelt a strong, savvy, world leader, who was working to advance not only the global aspirations of an emerging world power but the familiar, "down home" interests of everyday people.

Toward the end of his career, Roosevelt coined the term "New Nationalism," when he unsuccessfully sought to regain the Presidency as an independent, "Bull Moose" candidate. Again, his brand of nationalism did not just frame the interests of the nation in the world stage, but focused very much on the basic interests and needs of working class Americans.

As a self-described Progressive, Theodore Roosevelt set the stage for and inspired his distant cousin Franklin Roosevelt, whose mission became to reassure Americans that he would bring them from the depths of the Great Depression with what he called The New Deal.

The United States moved from Roosevelt to Roosevelt, from Square Deal to New Deal in a generation, wherein the

United States saw itself change from an emerging economic and military power to an economic basket case. By the early 1930s, about one in four American workers were unemployed, and the manufacturing sector had been gutted, losing about one third of its capacity. Banks were failing, and unprecedented numbers of farmers faced bankruptcy.

Economists continue to argue in studious and technical terms about whether President Franklin Roosevelt's New Deal helped lift the nation from The Great Depression, or helped prolong the depression and its drag on the economy. It's generally agreed, now, that the economy bottomed in 1932 then began a slow, inadequate recovery through the mid-1930s before sliding into recession in 1937-1938. The U.S. economy did not achieve full recovery until the U.S. created new industrial and production capacity to fight the Second World War.

Yet even while economists argue about the economic legacy, most people agree that the political legacy of Roosevelt's New Deal is most profoundly and lastingly established in America's working class. And for many of them, the economists' arguments are immaterial or beside the point. Like his cousin before him, Franklin Roosevelt redrew the American political map. But he charted a landscape that was populated and shaped by average working people to an even greater extent than Theodore Roosevelt had accomplished. FDR's map of the landscape reflected a working class constituency that expanded to include office workers, farmers, factory workers, and even the chronically unemployed. America was being inspired to see itself as a nation of people who were building, making and growing things – in stark contrast to what had been a nation of people who were watching and waiting, anxiously.

In his final campaign, just months before he died, Roosevelt said this in an October 1944 address at Soldier Field in Chicago: "America must remain the land of high wages and efficient production. Every full-time job in America must provide enough for a decent living. And that goes for jobs in mines, offices, factories, stores and canneries – everywhere where men and women are employed."[213]

I invite any consultant, marketing firm, political scientist or candidate for public office to test that statement with a working class "focus group" from any state in the Union. Let me know if there is any word or thought that they dispute or question.

The language is not lofty, and the ideal is one that – no matter how difficult it is to achieve – can be grasped and held by every American who counts on a paycheck to survive. It contains a healthy amount of political idealism, but it is grounded in the bricks and mortar of our society and our economy. Reading it now, more than 60 years later, it is easy to understand why Franklin Roosevelt is an iconic figure among much of our country's working class.

And in our own time we may, if we choose, hold up these statements from one of his last campaign speeches and ask ourselves if they have a place in the campaign speeches of our own time.

But if Roosevelt succeeded in bringing the working class to the fore of American politics, he also divided the electorate along lines that persisted for decades. Writing in Public Opinion Quarterly, Matthew Baum and Samuel Kernell wrote, "Indeed, from the mid-1930s until Pearl Harbor, the electorate arguably realigned its partisan loyalties more dramatically than at any other time in American history, and it did so almost exclusively on the basis of economic class."[214]

The writers reviewed a number of sources and analyzed some of George Gallup's earliest public opinion research to reach some interesting conclusions regarding Roosevelt's public support. In what they describe as a contentious political environment, Roosevelt averaged a 65 percent approval rating as he won three re-election campaigns.[215]

Prior to the emergence of war as the dominant issue in 1940, Roosevelt's approval rating among low income Americans averaged 57 percent, compared to 46 percent for medium income and 34 percent for high income Americans.[216]

It was this Roosevelt alignment that persisted for decades, giving rise to a host of political assumptions that would not be questioned until the ascendancy of Republican Ronald Reagan in the 1980 election, and the unanticipated emergence of what came to be called his "Reagan Democrats."

It is noteworthy to focus on international trade in the Reagan Administration when considering the loyalty of these crossover Democrats, and especially the working class interests among them.

Ideologically, Reagan was disposed to support free trade. In contrast to Franklin Roosevelt's reputation, Reagan was reluctant to assume for the government the inherent ability to "fix" markets that might not be operating at peak efficiency or bringing maximum benefits to workers.

But as Franklin Roosevelt did with fascism, Ronald Reagan conveyed to American voters that he intended for America to stand up for its interests in the world arena, especially in confronting the militarist and imperialist impulses of Communist states. Certainly Reagan's Cold War Realpolitik will pre-eminently define his legacy, but it is interesting to look at the United States' economic interests and at one particular episode that demonstrates the President's commitment to advancing his country's interests in global trade.

As in our own time, the U.S. economy was rebounding from recession by the end of the first Reagan term. Unfortunately as we also see today, the trade deficit was growing at an unacceptable rate. But this was before the Clinton-Bush era free trade agreements, and the reaction in Congress to the spiraling trade deficit was quite different. *The Economist* noted that almost 100 protectionist bills were drafted in 1985 in response to the trade deficit, and Japan came to symbolize the root causes of U.S. trade imbalances.[217]

Although the Plaza Accord does not occupy a prominent place in the minds of working class Americans, it stands as a monument of good old fashioned American public policy in global politics – and I am not sure we have seen the equal of it since.

Working through what was then the G-5,[218] the various governments hammered out a process to devalue the dollar relative to Japanese yen and German mark and thereby begin to address trade imbalances. This currency revaluation helped reverse growing trade deficits with European trading partners. The Plaza Accord presented Japanese manufacturers with compelling monetary and economic reasons to shift production capacity to the U.S., which helped drive growing employment in this sector into the 1990s.

President Reagan reiterated his vision in the wake of the acceptance of the Plaza Accord: "To make the international trading system work, all must abide by the rules."[219]

Reagan continued: "I believe that if trade is not fair for all, then trade is free in name only. I will not stand by and watch American businesses fail because of unfair trading practices abroad. I will not stand by and watch American workers lose their jobs because other nations do not play by the rules."[220] Yet the conventional wisdom today has become to keep economic nationalism at bay and keep elected officials docile and compliant, even in the face of record trade deficits and the loss of millions of manufacturing jobs.

In the meantime the struggle for America's soul has already begun with regard to free trade and protectionism. President Reagan and the Plaza Accord present an example from our recent past worth considering. Reagan was a chief executive who was a true believer in free trade, but who recognized that distorted currency values, coupled with massive trade imbalances and current accounts deficits, can undermine a nation's economy and the whole global trade system.

Conventional wisdom tells us that today's new political balances and power structures make a latter-day Plaza Accord unlikely. The Chinese are too powerful and their illegal tactics are becoming more effective. The Japanese still blame the agreement for a decade-long recession. The G-5 has expanded to include nations that are unwilling to negotiate any agreement that might be perceived primarily as in the interests of the United States.

Against this backdrop it is Ronald Reagan's confident assertiveness that stands out:

> We will vigorously pursue our policy of promoting free and open markets in this country and around the world. We will insist that all nations face up to their responsibilities of preserving and enhancing free trade everywhere. But let no one mistake our resolve to oppose any and all unfair trading practices. It is wrong for the American worker and American businessman to continue to bear the burden imposed by those who abuse the world trading system.[221]

Both those who admired him and those who competed with him recognized his stature and his commitment. And perhaps the working men and women of his own country recognized it as well. Our domestic political scene is primed for the emergence of a similar leader, particularly as trends in jobs, wages and benefits continue to erode our standard of living and our sense of security.

It is a tall order for the U.S. federal government to put our economic house in order and restore balance to trade. It requires strong domestic leadership to deal with federal fiscal deficits, historically low (or non-existent) savings rates among Americans, record trade deficits, and record debt among many sectors of society.

144

It also requires strong leadership on the international stage. America and Americans are not quite sure where they want to go in the world. A century after Theodore Roosevelt we are uncertain whether we want to project our military power in a dramatic and far-reaching way. More than 60 years after Franklin Roosevelt many workers are deeply insecure about the future of their livelihoods and the direction government should move in addressing the problem. Nearly 20 years after Ronald Reagan left office we are not sure whether we have the willpower, the ways and means to engage in a new global political struggle while getting our own economic house in order.

The free trade agreements that we signed so confidently after Reagan left office now hang over our economy like a massive doubt. Boosters and true believers hawk statistics to win over the hearts and minds of working men and women to the free trade cause. Opponents echo Ross Perot and trot out their own flip charts, facts and figures.

As with so many other issues affecting the working class, our 50:50, back-and-forth balance of power between Republicans and Democrats makes the whole ship seem subject to the latest gusts, but without a clear map.

In 2005 the CAFTA vote became a Moment of Truth or a Day of Reckoning for many in Congress. CAFTA (and other free trade agreements by association) were essentially put on trial in the House of Representatives. And a large measure of that guilt or innocence hinges on the damage done to American workers.

The ratification of NAFTA opened a chapter in the U.S. economy that has continued through three Presidential terms and through more than one shift in the balance of power in the two houses of Congress. When CAFTA escaped death by just one vote we may have seen the closing of that chapter.

But here is what has not happened. The hurdles and problems that working class Americans must overcome arise from many parts of the economy and many areas of policy. Trade agreements comprise just one category. Enforcement of trade laws is a key also. We do not have our fiscal and trade deficits in hand. We do not control our energy destiny, making our economy hostage to excessive energy price volatility and supply interruptions. We have failed to create a globally competitive tax structure that is designed to benefit our products in the world market – in stark contrast to many of our trading partners. We do not adequately train and educate our workforce.

Taken together, these matters present our workers with profound problems and serious limitations. But our elected leaders have not combined them effectively in a platform to inspire and unite America's working class.

I have said we must broaden our scope and sharpen our focus. The future success of American leadership depends on broadening the scope of concerns and policies to encompass the entire working class – male, female, black, white, urban, rural, old, young, whatever.

And this means presenting the issues in new ways. Just as we should resist the temptation to slice and dice our electorate too much, we should look to the diverse issues of the day and ask, "How can we connect these or weave these together to create a comprehensive and integrated agenda to put the working class back on solid ground in the middle class?"

That's right: Solid ground.

If we fail to attempt this we risk widening the gap between the middle class and much of the working class. We have arrived at the point where we must seriously ponder the consequences to our economy and our society if the door to the middle class is closed to much of the working class.

We risk the alienation of the working class from the American Dream. And from this comes disenchantment, cynicism and a loss of unity – none of which the United States can afford in today's competitive (and some would say dangerous) world.

The issues are broad and diverse enough to engage and unite a significant portion of the working class. The challenge comes in sharpening the focus of both the message and its delivery. To date, national candidates have been unable to frame the issues under the compelling banner of a "Square Deal" or "New Deal."

This is why so many working Americans perceive that the only deal available to them now is a Raw Deal.

Working class Americans may be excused also if they do not respond to the mixed messages of "tough on terrorism" but "soft on trade" in the world arena. In hindsight, Ronald Reagan's approach to both adversaries and allies on the global stage appears to be both stronger and more coherent to average Americans than what has been offered by recent leaders of both parties.

Yet everything is in place to create a platform that can rally the working class. The common planks are there. The tradition of a working class doorway to the middle class is there. The tradition of strong, assertive yet fair international leadership also is there.

What must now be done in the absence of a Roosevelt or a Reagan is to channel our energy at the grass roots. It begins with a willingness to identify key districts where the economic and demographic circumstances combine to make for a receptive and responsive audience. From there the challenges lie in the classic grassroots outreach and organization that bring voters, elected officials, interest groups and others under the banner.

To various extents some of this has already been happening. But the fate of the working class could still go in one of two directions.

Along one road the issues and the voters are not engaged, and the status quo of stagnant wages, atrophied benefits and exported jobs continues.

Along another road the issues are brought together and the voters join in a movement that is more powerful than the sum of its parts. Working class issues and working class voters determine the outcome of elections across the country. American society sees itself awakening to a working class renaissance.

The effects will be earth-shaking.

I would like to close with the words of Dr. Martin Luther King: "I say to you today, my friends . . . even though we face the difficulties of today and tomorrow, I still have a dream. It is a dream deeply rooted in the American dream. I have a dream that one day this nation will rise up . . . ."[222] Like Dr. King, I refuse "to believe that there are insufficient funds in the great vaults of opportunity of this nation."[223] Together the working men and women of this country working with an informed and concerned group of elected officials can meet and overcome the great challenges of the globalized economy.

WORKS CITED

[1] DR. KATE BONFENBRENNER & DR. STEPHANIE LUCE, THE CHANGING NATURE OF CORPORATE GLOBAL RESTRUCTURING: THE IMPACT OF PRODUCTION SHIFTS ON JOBS IN THE US, CHINA, AND AROUND THE GLOBE, REPORT TO THE US-CHINA ECONOMIC AND SECURITY REVIEW COMMISSION at i (Oct. 14, 2004).

[2] *Id.*

[3] *Id.*

[4] *Id.*

[5] *Id.* at ii.

[6] Sharon Brown & James Spletzer, U.S. Bureau of Labor Statistics, Labor Market Dynamics Associated with Movement of Work Overseas, Prepared for the November 15-16 OECD Conference "The Globalisation of Production," at 5 (Nov. 2, 2005).

[7] BONFENBRENNER & LUCE, *supra* note 1, at iii.

[8] U.S. Chamber of Commerce, *Get the Facts*, THETRUECOSTS.ORG, at http://www.thetruecosts.org (last visited Nov. 27, 2006).

[9] Labor Research Association, *Low-Wage Nation*, LRA ONLINE (June 22, 2006), at http://www.laborresearch.org.

[10] Economic Policy Institute, *Wage Growth Slows for Most Workers Between 2000 and 2005*, ECONOMIC SNAPSHOTS (Jan. 11, 2006), at http://www.epi.org.

[11] *Id.*

[12] *Id.*

[13] *Id.*

[14] *See generally* National Association of Manufacturers, *The NAM Annual Labor Day Report: Energy Costs: Shrinking the Pie for America's Workers* (Sept. 2006).

[15] *Id.* at 16.

[16] *Id.*

[17] LAWRENCE MISHEL, ECONOMIC POLICY INSTITUTE, POLICY MEMORANDUM: WHAT'S WRONG WITH THE ECONOMY 1(June 12, 2006).

[18] LAWRENCE MISHEL, JARED BERNSTEIN, AND SYLVIA ALLEGRETTO, ECONOMIC POLICY INSTITUTE, THE STATE OF WORKING AMERICA: 2006/2007, at 251 (2006 ed.).

19 *Id.*

20 Irwin Stelzer, Senior Fellow and Director of Economic Policy Studies for the Hudson Institute, *The Times They Are A-Changin'*, HUDSON INSTITUTE (Aug. 14, 2006), at http://www.hudson.org.

21 SARAH ANDERSON ET AL., EXECUTIVE EXCESS 2005: DEFENSE CONTRACTORS GET MORE BUCKS FOR THE BANG 4 (12th ed., Aug. 30, 2005).

22 *Id.* at 13.

23 Press Release, U.S. Census Bureau, *Income Climbs, Poverty Stabilizes, Uninsured Rate Increases* (Aug. 28, 2006).

24 *Id.*

25 *Id.*

26 *Id.*

27 *Id.*

28 Labor Research Association, *supra* note 9.

29 Economic Policy Institute, *Facts and Figures From the State of Working America 2006/2007: Jobs* (Sept. 2006).

30 Economic Policy Institute, *Facts and Figures From the State of Working America 2006/2007: Family Income* (Sept. 2006).

31 *Id.*

32 *Id.*

33 Economic Policy Institute, *Facts and Figures From the State of Working America 2006/2007: Work Hours* (Sept. 2006).

34 Economic Policy Institute, *Facts and Figures From the State of Working America 2006/2007: Health Care & Pensions* (Sept. 2006).

35 *Id.*

36 *Id.*

37 Labor Research Association, *The Slowdown Hits U.S. Workers*, LRA ONLINE: THE ECONOMY (June 30, 2006), *at* http://www.laborresearch.org.

38 Board of Governors of the Federal Reserve System, Monetary Policy Report to the Congress 5 (Feb. 15, 2006).

39 *Id.* at 7.

[40] *Id.*

[41] Press Release, U.S. Bureau of Economic Analysis, *Personal Income and Outlays: September 2006* (Oct. 30, 2006).

[42] *Id.*

[43] Labor Research Association, *supra* note 37.

[44] Board of Governors of the Federal Reserve System, *supra* note 38, at 6.

[45] *Id.* at 2.

[46] Dr. David LeReah, Chief Economist, National Association of Realtors, *Real Estate Reality Check* (Aug. 17-18, 2006).

[47] *Id.*

[48] *Id.*

[49] *Id.*

[50] *Id.*

[51] *Id.*

[52] *Id.*

[53] Noelle Knox, *Job Losses Lead to Drop in Home Prices; Hard-hit Danville, Ill., Area Sees Prices Fall 11% in 2nd Quarter*, USA TODAY, at Money 1B (Aug. 16, 2006).

[54] DR. LESLIE HOSSFELD ET AL., THE ECONOMIC AND SOCIAL IMPACT OF JOB LOSS IN ROBESON COUNTY, NORTH CAROLINA 1993 – 2003 (Aug. 2004).

[55] *Id.* at 4.

[56] *Id.*

[57] *Id.* at 5-6.

[58] *Id.* at 6.

[59] *Id.* at 9.

[60] *Id.* at 12.

[61] *Id.* at 7.

[62] *Id.* at 8.

[63] DR. LESLIE HOSSFELD ET AL., *supra* note 54, at 10.

[64] *Id.* at 11.

[65] DR. M. HARVEY BRENNER, ESTIMATING THE EFFECTS OF ECONOMIC CHANGE ON NATIONAL HEALTH AND SOCIAL WELL-BEING: A STUDY (U.S. Government Printing Office, U.S. Congress 1984).

[66] Dr. Glen O. Jenson, *Unemployment and the Family*, PENPAGES (College of Ag. Scis., Penn State Univ., Dec.1, 1999).

[67] *Id.*

[68] *Id.*

[69] Ariel Kalil & Kathleen M. Ziol-Guest, *Parental Job Loss and Children's Academic Progress in Two-Parent Families*, 23-24, presented at 2003-2004 Census Bureau Research Development Grants Conference, Joint Center for Poverty Research, Northwestern University/University of Chicago (Sept. 9, 2004).

[70] W. Jean Yeung & Sandra L. Hofferth, *Family Adaptations to Income and Job Loss in The U.S.*, 19(3) J. Fam. & Econ. Issues 255 (1998).

[71] *Id.*

[72] *Id.*

[73] *Id.*

[74] Press Release, American Psychological Association, *Job Loss and the Resulting Financial Strain Can Lead to Downward Spiral of Depression and Poor Health, Says Research* (Oct. 6, 2002), *available at* http://www.apa.org/releases/unemployment.html.

[75] Fact Sheet, Family Adaptation to Occupational Loss Project, Center on the Family, University of Hawaii at Manoa, *Stresses & Changes in the Face of Job Loss* (Apr. 1997).

[76] *Id.*

[77] DR. JON HONECK, POLICY MATTERS OHIO, INTERNATIONAL TRADE AND JOB LOSS IN OHIO, 5-6 (Feb. 2004).

[78] Dr. Peter Morici, *Economy Adds 75,000 Jobs in May – Growth Slowing in Second Quarter*, ROBERT H. SMITH SCHOOL OF BUSINESS NEWS AND EVENTS (June 5, 2006). Morici contends: "Unemployment fell to 4.6 percent largely because more adults chose to not participate in the job market. The adult labor force participation rate remains significantly lower than when George Bush took over stewardship of the economy. If adults were participating in the job market at 2000 levels, 2.7 million more people would

be looking for work and unemployment would exceed 6 percent."

79 Dr. N. Gregory Mankiw, Chairman, Council of Economic Advisors, Remarks to the National Economists Club and Society of Government Economists (February 17, 2004).

80 *Building Blue-Collar . . . Burgers?*, CBS NEWS (Feb. 20, 2004).

81 Jacobellis v. Ohio, 378 U.S. 184, 197 (1964)(Stewart, J., concurring).

82 Michael Zweig, *Six Points on Class*, 58(3) MONTHLY REVIEW (July/Aug. 2006).

83 *Id.*

84 *Id.*

85 David Moberg, *America's Forgotten Majority: Why the White Working Class Still Matters. – Review – Book Review*, THE PROGRESSIVE (Sept. 2000).

86 *Id.*

87 Zweig, *supra* note 82.

88 *See generally*, Richard F. Hamilton, *The Marginal Middle Class: A Reconsideration*, 31(2) AMERICAN SOCIOLOGICAL REVIEW 192 (Apr. 1966).

89 *Id..*

90 The Harris Poll, #24, *Outsourcing of U.S. Jobs Abroad Very Unpopular* (Apr. 7, 2004).

91 *Id.*

92 *Id.*

93 *Id.*

94 *Id.*

95 *Id.*

96 Pew Research Center for the People and the Press, *Beyond Red vs. Blue: Republicans Divided About Role of Government – Democrats by Social and Personal Values* (May 10, 2005).

97 *Id.*

98 *Id.*

99 *Id.*

100 *Id.*

101 *Id.*

102 *Id.*
103 *Id.*
104 *Id.*
105 *Id.*
106 *Id.*
107 WORD SPY, http://www.wordspy.com.
108 *Soccer Mom*, WORD SPY, (Jan. 16, 1999), *at*
http://www.wordspy.com/words/soccermom.asp
109 *Id.*
110 *Id.*
111 Ben Klayman, *Cracks Appear in NASCAR Voters'
Republican Loyalty*, REUTERS (Aug. 17, 2006).
112 *Id.*
113 Jeffrey Birnbaum & Chris Cilliza, '*Mortgage Moms' May
Star in Midterm Vote*, WASHINGTON POST, A01 (Sept. 5
2006).
114 *Id.*
115 *Matthew* 23:24.
116 *11th Congressional District Candidate Q&A*, ASHEVILLE
CITIZEN-TIMES (Oct. 15, 2006).
117 Shuler for Congress, *Charles Taylor, available at*
http://www.heathshuler.com/HS-Again.mov.
118 Alex Brown, *Ellsworth Defeats Hostettler*, Indiana
Statesman, Campus Section (Nov. 8, 2006).
119 Peter Roskam, Remarks at Addison Candidate Forum
(Aug. 9, 2006).
120 *Dean Touts a 'Jesus Strategy'*, The Washington Times
(Dec. 26, 2003).
121 The Democratic Leadership Council sponsored just such a
working conference in 2003 to address how to "seize the
cultural center." Press Release, Democratic Leadership
Council, God, Guns, and Guts: Seizing the Cultural Center
(Oct. 16, 2003).
122 Jonathan Kaplan, *The NASCAR Voter That Never Was*,
THE HILL (Oct. 13, 2004).
123 Steve Cahalan, *Group Highlights Trade, Job Loss*, LA
CROSSE TRIBUNE (Sept. 29, 2004).

[124] Jim Jontz, *Bleeding Ohio: Can the Politics of Trade Change Red States to Blue?* (Jan. 13, 2005).

[125] Press Release, Manufacturers Association of Central New York, MACNY, Local Manufacturers Team-Up to Highlight Plight of the U.S. Worker (Oct. 25, 2006).

[126] *Id.*

[127] Marilyn H. Karfield, *Ohio Clergy City Key Role of Religion in Politics*, CLEVELAND JEWISH NEWS (Oct. 27, 2006).

[128] *Revelations* 3:15-16.

[129] THOMAS E. PATTERSON, THE VANISHING VOTER: CIVIC INVOLVEMENT IN AN AGE OF UNCERTAINTY (Alfred A. Knopf Publishers, Sept. 2002).

[130] *Id.*

[131] *Id.*

[132] Press Release, U.S. Census Bureau, U.S. Voter Turnout Up in 2004, Census Bureau Reports (May 26, 2005).

[133] *Id.*

[134] *Id.*

[135] *Id.*

[136] *Id.*

[137] *Id.*

[138] *Id.*

[139] *Id.*

[140] *Id.*

[141] *Id.*

[142] *Id.*

[143] *Id.*

[144] ABRAHAM MASLOW, A THEORY OF HUMAN MOTIVATION (1943).

[145] J. Finkelstein, *Maslow's Hierarchy of Needs*, Wikipedia (Oct. 27, 2006).

[146] WNBC/Marist Poll, New York State: Campaign 2006 (July 19, 2006).

[147] *Id.*

[148] *Id.*

[149] *Id.*

[150] *Id.*

[151] *Id.*

[152] U.S. Census Bureau, 2005 American Community Survey, (2006).

[153] U.S. Bureau of Economic Analysis, *supra* note 41.

[154] Press Release, U.S. Senator Lindsey Graham, Senators Graham and Clinton Launch Manufacturing Caucus (June 14, 2005).

[155] Tim Whitmire, *1 House Victory Offers Strategy for Dems,* ASSOCIATED PRESS (Nov. 11, 2006). The article does not specify who the other victorious Democrat was, but would be either Ron Klein in Florida's 22nd District, or John Yarmuth in Kentucky's 3rd District.

[156] The remainder identified themselves as retired.

[157] U.S. Census Bureau, *supra* note 152.

[158] INDIANA INSTITUTE FOR WORKING FAMILIES, THE STATUS OF WORKING FAMILIES IN INDIANA: 2006 UPDATE, *Highlights* (Sept. 2006).

[159] The remainder identified themselves as retired.

[160] Press Release, Keystone Research Center, Income Inequality Grew in Pennsylvania Over the Past Two Decades (Jan. 26, 2006).

[161] *Id.*

[162] *Id.*

[163] *Id.*

[164] *Id.*

[165] Alissa Anderson Garcia, California Budget Project, *California's Job Growth Was Strong, But Wage Gains Were Weak Between 2003 and 2005,* POLICY POINTS (Aug. 2006).

[166] *Id.*

[167] *Id.*

[168] George W. Bush, Press Conference (Nov. 8, 2006).

[169] Tim Storey, *Election 2006 – No Party for the GOP?,* STATE LEGISLATURES (Sept. 2006).

[170] National Council of State Legislatures, *Democrats Make Major Gains in Nation's State Legislatures, at* http://www.ncsl.org/programs/press/2006/pr061108.htm (last updated Nov. 14, 2006).

[171] Data collected from Polling Report, Election 2004, at http://www.pollingreport.com/cong2004.htm (last visited Nov. 14, 2006).

[172] Ipsos-Public Affairs Poll (Dec. 17-19,2004).

[173] Data collected from Polling Report, Election 2006, at http://www.pollingreport.com/2006a.htm (last visited Nov. 14, 2006); data collected from Polling Report, Election 2004, *supra* note 171.

[174] Fox News/Opinion Dynamics Poll (Aug. 30-31, 2005); CNN/USA Today/Gallup Poll (Oct. 13-16, 2005); CNN/USA Today/Gallup Poll (Nov. 11-13, 2005).

[175] Data collected from Polling Report, Election 2006, *supra* note 173.

[176] *Id.*

[177] *Id.*

[178] Data collected from RealClearPolitics, 2006 Generic Congressional Vote Polls, at http://www.realclearpolitics.com/polls/archive/?poll_id=14 (last visited Nov. 14, 2006); Data collected from Polling Report, Election 2004, *supra* note 171.

[179] Data collected from Polling Report, Election 2004, *supra* note 171.

[180] Data collected by averaging all reported polls collected by RealClearPolitics, 2006 Generic Congressional Vote Polls, at http://www.realclearpolitics.com/polls/archive/?poll_id=14 (last visited Nov. 14, 2006).

[181] *Id.*

[182] ABC News/Washington Post Poll (Aug. 3-6, 2006).

[183] *Id.*

[184] Data collected from Polling Report, Election 2006, *supra* note 173.

[185] *Id.*

[186] Pew Research Center for the People and the Press Survey (Nov. 1-4, 2006); Pew Research Center for the People and the Press Survey (Oct. 17-22, 2006); Pew Research Center for the People and the Press Survey (Sept. 21-Oct. 4, 2006); Pew Research Center for the People and the Press Survey (Sept.

6-10, 2006); Pew Research Center for the People and the Press Survey (Aug. 9-13, 2006).

[187] K.A. Dixon et al., *At a Crossroads: American Workers Assess Jobs and Economic Security Amid the Race for Preisdent*, 7(3) WORK TRENDS 14 (Oct. 2004).

[188] *Id.* at 1-2.

[189] *Id.* at 8.

[190] Press Release, International Association of Machinists and Aerospace Workers, Workers in Four Big States Say 'Job Crisis' Far From Over (May 3, 2004).

[191] International Association of Machinists and Aerospace Workers (2004).

[192] *Id.*

[193] *Id.*

[194] *Id.*

[195] *Id.*

[196] Nationwide exit polling by the National Election Pool, which consists of ABC, AP, CBS, CNN, FOX, NBC, and is conducted by Edison/Mitofsky (Nov. 7, 2006).

[197] *Id.*

[198] U.S. Bureau of Labor Statistics.

[199] U.S. Census Bureau, *supra* note 152.

[200] *Id.*

[201] CENTER FOR TAX AND BUDGET ACCOUNTABILITY & NORTHERN ILLINOIS UNIVERSITY, THE STATE OF WORKING ILLINOIS: EXECUTIVE SUMMARY (Nov. 17, 2005).

[202] Roskam, *supra* note 119.

[203] *See* Ken Jennings & Jeffrey W. Steagall, *Unions and NAFTA's Legislative Passage: Confrontation and Cover*, 21(1) Labor Studies Journal 61, 64 (Mar. 22, 1996).

[204] *Id.*

[205] Steve Neal, *A Love of Labor for Gore*, CHICAGO SUN-TIMES, at 47 (Oct. 6, 2000).

[206] Jennings & Steagall, *supra* note 202 at 64.

[207] *Id.* at 67.

[208] Robyn Meredith, *Giant Sucking Sound*, FORBES (Sept. 29, 2003).

[209] Brian Bremner, *EDS: Getting Out Front in Outsourcing*, BUSINESSWEEK (June 26, 2006).

[210] *Id.*

[211] Letter from Theodore Roosevelt to Sir Edward Gray (Nov. 15, 1913).

[212] Theodore Roosevelt, Remarks at the New York State Fair, Syracuse, New York (Sept. 7, 1903).

[213] President Franklin D. Roosevelt, Address at Soldiers' Field, Chicago, Illinois (Oct. 28, 1944).

[214] Matthew A. Baum & Samuel Kernell, *Economic Class and Popular Support for Franklin Roosevelt in War and Peace*, 65 PUBLIC OPINION QUARTERLY 198, 199 (2001).

[215] *Id.* at 202.

[216] *Id.* at 206.

[217] *Reaganomics Redux: Why the World Cannot Count on a Repeat of the 1980s*, THE ECONOMIST (Sept. 18, 2003).

[218] The Ministers of Finance and Central Bank Governors of France, the Federal Republic of Germany, Japan, the United Kingdom, and the United States.

[219] President Ronald Reagan, Remarks at a White House Meeting With Business and Trade Leaders (Sept. 23, 1985).

[220] *Id.*

[221] *Id.*

[222] Dr. Martin Luther King, Address at the Lincoln Memorial, *I Have a Dream* (Aug. 28, 1963).

[223] *Id.*

Tom Mullikin

As a senior attorney and environmental expert with the Charlotte law firm of Moore & Van Allen, PLLC, Tom leads the firm's Government, Policy and Regulatory Affairs Team. His practice focuses on corporate compliance, regulatory relations and legislative representation. Tom's career spans more than twenty years and includes key legislative staff roles, lobbying activities, extensive environmental legal representation and management of environmental, energy and healthcare issue campaigns for industry. He previously served as Chief Counsel and Vice President for Public Affairs to the largest environmental services company in the world.

He has served on state and congressional staffs as well as an advisor and campaign manager to senior members of Congress and U.S. Presidential candidates from both the Republican and Democratic parties.

Tom led a team of researchers and environmental experts on an expedition to Antarctica in late 2005 to study the effects of climate change on the polar regions. He produced a subsequent video documentary, entitled: *Climate Change: Global Problems, Global Solutions* which has received widespread acclaim in both business and environmental circles. In October 2006, he led a second team to Namibia, Africa, to follow up on the findings of the Antarctica expedition and further explore the impact of global climate change on the fragile Sub-Saharan environment.

Tom has been widely published in both legal and mainstream periodicals, including *Campaigns and Elections Magazine, South Carolina Jurisprudence, Vital Speeches of the Day, UCLA Journal of Environmental Law and Policy and Georgetown International Environmental Law Review,* and has been quoted as an expert in both the law and the environment by *The Los Angeles Times, Newsday, The St. Petersburg (Fla.) Times, The Charlotte Observer, The Rocky Mountain News, The Salt Lake Tribune,* and *Huntinamibia.*

http://www.mvalaw.com

www.ingramcontent.com/pod-product-compliance
Lightning Source LLC
Chambersburg PA
CBHW021828020426
42334CB00014B/531

9 780979 017834